KW-471-123

Contents

VI

List of Tables

Abbreviations

AIC	ASEAN Industrial Complementation
AIJV	ASEAN Industrial Joint Venture
AIP	ASEAN Industrial Projects
ASEAN	Association of Southeast Asian Nations
CACEU	Central African Customs and Economic Union (alternatively: UDEAC Union Douanière et Economique de l'Afrique Centrale)
CACM	Central American Common Market (alternatively: MCCA Mercado Común Centroamericano)
CAR	Central African Republic
CARICOM	Caribbean Community
CARIFTA	Caribbean Free Trade Association
CFA	Communauté Financière Africaine
CUWAS	Customs Union of West African States (alternatively: UDEAO Union Douanière des Etats de l'Afrique de l'Ouest)
EAC	East African Community
ECCAS	Economic Community of Central African States (alternatively: CEEAC Communauté Economique des Etats de l'Afrique Centrale)
ECLA	Economic Commission for Latin America
ECO	Economic Co-operation Organization
ECOWAS	Economic Community of West African States (alternatively: CEDEAO Communauté Economique des Etats de l'Afrique de l'Quest)
ECU	Equatorial Customs Union (alternatively: UDE Union Douanière Equatoriale)
EEC	European Economic Community
GCC	Gulf Co-operation Council
GDP	Gross Domestic Product
GNP	Gross National Product
GSP	Generalised System of Preferences
IMF	International Monetary Fund
JPE	Joint Purpose Enterprise
LAFTA	Latin American Free Trade Association (alternatively: ALALC Asociacion Latinoamericana de Libre Comercio)
LAIA	Latin American Integration Association (alternatively: ALADI Asociacion Latinoamericana de Integracion)
MFA	Multi Fibre Agreement
NTB	Nontariff Barrier
OAU	Organisation of African Unity
OEC	Organisation for Economic Co-operation and Development
PTA	Preferential Trade Area for Eastern and Southern African States; Preferential Trading Arrangement of ASEAN
PTACU	PTA Currency Units
RCD	Regional Co-operation for Development
R&D	Research and Development

RIDC	Regional Integration among Developing Countries
SAARC	South Asian Association for Regional Co-operation
SACU	Southern African Customs Union
SADCC	Southern African Development Coordination Conference
TB	Tariff Barrier
TCR	Taxe de Coopération Régionale
UNCTAD	United Nations Conference on Trade and Development
UNDP	United Nations Development Programme
WAEC	West African Economic Community
	(alternatively: CEAO Communauté Economique de l'Afrique de l'Quest)

Preface

The recent economic policy debate in developing countries has been characterized by a renewed interest in regional economic integration as a means of stimulating growth and facilitating structural adjustment. In particular, in Sub-Saharan Africa and Latin America several attempts have been made to revitalize existing integration schemes and to create new ones. Against this background, the purpose of this study is to evaluate the economic rationale of various integration attempts, to review the experience with major integration schemes and their operation over the last thirty years, and to provide suggestions for successful regional cooperation.

The analysis presented in the study expands and updates earlier work by Rolf J. Langhammer. It has greatly benefited from collaboration with the World Bank. Vinod Thomas, Kazi Matin and Andràs Inotai provided intellectual support, useful background material and helpful comments on an earlier draft. Their assistance is gratefully acknowledged.

Thanks are also due to Ingrid Lawaetz for the careful typing of the final manuscript. Bernhard Klein and Sylvia Künne of the editing staff deserve credit for painstakingly preparing the manuscript for publication.

Kiel, May 1990   Horst Siebert

A. Concepts and Definitions

For almost three decades regional integration among developing countries (RIDC) has been on the agenda of their governments. Though it often remained open whether regional integration should serve as an instrument or should be the target itself, perceptions were mostly af-firmative: voices opting against regional integration were rare and almost all politicians argued that cooperation - another catchword for region-alism - was per se conducive to economic development of individual mem-ber countries.

Historically, it has mainly been the group of Latin American coun-tries which has taken a positive stance towards privileges and preferen-ces for neighbouring countries since the 1950s. In Latin America, re-gional integration was mainly intended to surmount the limits to import substitution in narrow domestic markets and to gain competitiveness before meeting the challenges of world markets.

In Sub-Saharan Africa the point of departure was completely differ-ent. Large colonial entities were split into politically independent but economically very fragile units which inherited a large number of common instruments and institutions such as language, tax systems, tariffs, currencies, physical infrastructure, to mention but some of them. What was largely missing was a network of interstate communication and trans-portation so that natural protection of small local industries in the newly founded states remained high. Contrary to Latin America, there was a high level of institutional integration in Sub-Saharan Africa at inde-pendence which was threatened by the priority of the new governments for nation-building and national autonomy.

Historical patterns in the Middle East and Asia were again different from those in the two other regions. Given the extreme heterogeneity of the countries in terms of market size, resource endowment and level of income as well as their often conflicting positions in political ideologies and economic order systems, common economic targets were very difficult to define. Conflicts and divergences could be much more frequently observed than consensus and convergences. This holds both for compro-mising on positions towards third countries as well as for formulating common regional economic issues. Under such conditions, countries in the

Middle East and Asia have found it much more difficult to establish a platform for regionalism.

One of the characteristics of early approaches to regional integration has been the lack of conceptual clarity as well as the inappropriateness of concepts applied. As far as concepts were concerned, integration and cooperation often appeared as synonyms in arrangements of regional groupings and/or were simultaneously labelled as a process and as a status. However, a distinction has to be made between integration and cooperation [Balassa, 1976]: integration is a process aiming at abolishing discrimination between local and foreign goods, services, and factors. This process runs through at least four stages: free trade area, customs union, common market, and economic union. The sequence of these stages is not binding, but experience suggests to start integration by removing barriers to trade in goods (and services) between partner countries while each partner maintains its national tariff towards nonmember countries (free trade area). The second stage is based on the first one and comprises the harmonisation of national tariffs against third countries to a common external tariff (customs union). Liberalising the circulation of factors of production within the customs union then leads to a common market, while the harmonisation of remaining national economic policies characterises the fourth stage, the economic union. Finally, countries may opt for total economic integration with a supranational authority [Balassa, 1962, p. 2].

Contrary to integration, cooperation includes concerted actions aimed at lessening discrimination in certain areas of common interest. Cooperation is thus much more limited in scope than integration.

The second shortcoming has emerged from a "fallacy of transposition". The historically unique example of the integration process in the EEC between 1957 and 1968 when the first two stages of integration were implemented simultaneously served as a model. Governments of developing countries misunderstood this process as a case of limited cooperation without surrendering national sovereignty and tried to copy the example in their countries. However, many initial conditions conducive to integration in Europe had been overlooked by governments of developing countries: e.g. a high level of intraregional trade before integration was started; similarities in income and industrialisation levels allowing for intraindustry specialisation; political congeniality in foreign affairs; capability and willingness to provide compensation payments.

It has taken quite a long time for developing countries to accept the fallacy of transposition and to draw lessons. The intention of this study is to show why the European way to integration did not work in developing countries and which alternative avenues to integration have been pursued. The second chapter elaborates the rationale of regional integration and makes a distinction between expected economic benefits and those which were conceived as non-economic benefits. Chapter C scrutinises manifold barriers to integration (natural, political, economic, and politico-economic barriers). Chapter D highlights the empirical experience of major integration schemes by concentrating on recent trends and reasons for changes. Why most schemes failed to meet even modest expectations is summarised in Chapter E. Here again, political reasons for failure are given much attention in order to take account of the eminently political process of surrendering national sovereignty. In Chapter F, attempts are made to draw lessons from the experiences for the scope of RIDC and potential policy actions by bi- and multilateral donors.

B. The Rationale of Regional Integration among Developing Countries

I. Expected Economic Benefits

1. The "Training Ground" Argument

The Vinerian customs union theory [Viner, 1950] exposes two short-run "once and for all" effects of liberalising intraregional trade: the replacement of domestic production by imports from partner countries (trade creation) and the replacement of imports from nonmember countries by those from member countries (trade diversion). Both effects emerge as a result of liberalising trade among each other and from changing relative prices between imports from member and nonmember countries. Viner evaluated trade creation as welfare increasing and trade diversion as welfare reducing from a world welfare point of view. His theory provoked an extensive theoretical discussion on additional consumption and production effects of customs unions and alternative assessment criteria (a single country's versus the world's welfare). The result of this discussion was inconclusive: even a trade-diverting customs union could be welfare-increasing and a trade-creating union could be welfare-reducing.[1]

Policy makers in developing countries as well as many scholars dealing with RIDC dismissed the Vinerian conclusion as irrelevant for conditions prevailing in the Third World (e.g. because of idle capacities). They assessed intraregional trade expansion as per se beneficial and even advocated trade diversion.[2] Their main argument was an assumed positive effect of infant industry protection in a regional union on quality control, marketing techniques and other prerequisites for later success on world markets ("training ground" argument). This case for protecting in particular infant export activities was later on refined by Morawetz [1974]. He maintains that intraregional trade expansion can

---

[1] Cf. Gehrels [1956/57]; Johnson [b]; Lipsey [1957; 1960]; Meade [1955] and the review article of Krauss [1972].

[2] Cf. e.g. Linder [1966] or the review article of Jaber [1970] and the literature cited there.

promote intraindustrial specialisation through product diversification and thus may improve the competitiveness of extraregional exports.

2. Enlarging the Size of the Domestic Market and Achieving Economies of Scale

Reducing costs of investment per unit of output has often been mentioned as an important benefit of RIDC. Most scholars rate this dynamic effect of integration higher than the static trade effects.[1] Empirical studies for developed countries [Haldi, Whitcomb, 1967] as well as for developing countries seemed to support this argument, especially for relatively capital-intensive industries and for developing countries with small domestic markets.[2] The existence of scale economies has, however, been challenged by e.g. Kahnert et al. [1969, p. 22]. They mention various counterarguments such as marketing, distribution and transportation costs growing disproportionately with the size of output. Likewise, economies of scale might not be connected with the size of the plant but with the length of the production runs.

3. Improving Resource Allocation and Availability of Resources

To the extent that small domestic markets constrain economic growth, regional integration is looked upon as an instrument to make such a constraint less binding. An intraregional division of labour is expected to be more consistent with the comparative advantages of member countries without exposing their economies to the rough competition in world markets. In addition, RIDC is expected to promote growth by expanding the volume of investable funds, i.e. the availability of local private as well as public savings, and of foreign risk capital [Kahnert et al., 1969, p. 26 f.].

---

[1] Cf. the review by Vaitsos [1978].

[2] Cf. Carnoy [1972] for Latin American countries and Pearson, Ingram [1980] for the hypothetical case of integration among Ghana and the Ivory Coast.

Yet, the validity of these arguments crucially depends on the full utilisation of available resources. If resources are idle, the employment of these resources becomes the relevant problem and not the reallocation of employed resources. It is likely that in low-income countries this argument is much more relevant than in middle-income countries of the Latin American type. Thus, improving resource availability and allocation as a result of RIDC could mainly be expected for advanced developing countries with a high degree of resource utilisation. This reflects again the "fallacy of transposition" as resource utilisation was high in the case of the EEC.

4. Enhancing Industrialisation

Almost all developing countries have equated the expansion of the industrial base with rapid economic development. When domestic markets proved to be too small to allow efficient import substitution as the starting point of industrialisation, the formation of a regional market was seen as a way out of this impasse. In economic terms, developing countries have regarded industrialisation as a rational social choice, and they were willing to bear the costs of income foregone by not importing from the cheapest available source or by specialising in activities in which they do not have comparative advantages. Given this social preference for industrialisation anything that lowers the cost of additional industrial capacity increases welfare and contributes to the countries' development [Johnson, a, pp. 208-210; Cooper, Massell, 1965]. Compared to industrialisation on a domestic basis, RIDC lowers the opportunity costs of import substitution. The larger the social preference of a country is, the less important is the Vinerian welfare-reducing effect of trade diversion for countries entering a regional grouping. However, a problem associated with RIDC is that opening the domestic market to industrial imports from member countries entails a sacrifice of domestic industrial capacity foregone. Such a loss must then be compensated by reciprocal preferences for industrial products conceded by all member countries. A practical problem with reciprocity arises since each member country demands preferences for products in which it enjoys comparative advantages within the grouping. However, the relative resource endowment of participating countries might be such that some countries possess no or few industrial products which they could produce at lower prices than their neighbours but enjoy comparative advantages in nonindustrial products. Under these conditions preferences could not be negotiated on a mutual basis for the industrial sector. Furthermore, powerful member countries could exert pressure on weaker partners to provide a market for high-cost products of the powerful member without offering compensation in terms of mutual industrial preferences [Johnson, a, p. 209].

Summarising, if intraunion comparative advantages exist within the industrial sector rather than between the industrial and nonindustrial sectors, each partner may gain compared to the alternative of national industrialisation based on import substitution. Otherwise, countries may see their social preferences violated even if they would gain more in terms of income or expansion of nonindustrial activities than they lose in the industrial sector. From an economic point of view, the preference for industrialisation is a second-best objective and can, therefore, provoke distributional conflicts among partners. Such conflicts may be the larger, the more national resource endowments differ between partner countries and the more uneven the initial stage of industrialisation among member countries.

5. Joint Production of Public Goods

Joint production of public goods is a matter of cooperation, not of integration. The benefits obtained from cooperation in producing public goods depend on how the two constituent characteristics of public goods, nonexcludability and nonrivalry, can be operationalised. In a narrow sense, international cooperation is necessary only when pareto-relevant technological externalities exist, i.e. when production and/or utility functions of economic agents are interdependent (e.g. the exploitation of internationally mobile resources such as fish, the environment, radio waves and the space) and when interdependence results in pareto-sub-optimal market solutions (overfishing, overpollution). Existing integration schemes have not yet paid much attention to such public goods. Yet, recent developments since the establishment of the Law of the Sea suggest that existing integration schemes devote more interest to the joint exploitation of deep sea mineral resources, to fishing regulations but also to environmental resources labelled as "common heritage of mankind" such as wildlife protection.

Until now traditional integration schemes have concentrated more on joint production of borderline cases between public and private goods, such as joint public services, training, research and production and maintenance of physical infrastructure. In fact, products with a long gestation period, high capital coefficients and decreasing marginal costs are candidates for joint production as they promise large savings of costs for individual countries compared to parallel production on several protected national markets under national authority.

In many cases such goods are only available if supranational initiatives are launched. Yet, cooperation is susceptible to conflicts about a "fair" or "equal" distribution of benefits and costs, as well as about management and locational issues. Such conflicts may even be more pronounced than in an integration scheme since costs and benefits arising from cooperation are often tangible and pecuniary. At least costs of cooperation can be measured in a straightforward way and hence serve politicians as a clear-cut yardstick for assessing the preferability of participation. Joint production of public goods is particularly prone to conflicts if a distinction can be made between producing and consuming countries, e.g. in cases of dams, ports, and other immobile goods and services. Consuming countries will claim compensation for production effects foregone, e.g. in terms of privileges concerning access to management positions, purchase guarantees at preferential conditions, and exemptions from costs of maintenance. In total, success in the joint production of public goods is to achieve more easily when goods concerned are genuine public goods rather than disguised private ones.

6. Protection against Adverse Developments in World Markets

Benefits arising from a reduction of the external vulnerability of developing countries have mainly been envisaged for commodity export dependent countries [UNCTAD, d, p. 9]. Regional integration was hypothesised to foster structural change in production from the primary to the secondary sector and within exports towards manufactured goods.

Erratic price fluctuations in commodity markets would then be less detrimental for the import capacity and the planning conditions in the countries concerned.

Lewis [1980] has used a similar argument in a much wider context.
In his reasoning, slower growth and rising protectionism in developed
countries would require a new engine of growth for developing countries. Lewis believes that trade among developing countries in a broad
South-South preference scheme could provide such an engine. However,
this suggestion overlooks that protectionism and economic fluctuations
affect regional trade sometimes even more than trade with industrialised
countries because of distributional conflicts and political disputes. As a
result, an external vulnerability of individual countries applies to regional markets as much as to world markets.

II. Noneconomic Benefits

1. Improving the Collective Bargaining Power vis-à-vis Industrialised Countries

Raising the collective bargaining power vis-à-vis industrialised
countries is not an end to itself. It serves a purpose which can be of
economic and/or political nature. In economic terms, supply and demand
issues have to be dealt with separately. On the supply side, partners in
RIDC can engage themselves in concerted actions in primary commodity
markets, in forming mini-cartels in order to gain monopoly rents, in
jointly demanding better access to markets of industrialised countries. As
neighbouring countries tend to belong to the same climatic belts and/or
to the same geological areas, the probability that they supply homogeneous agricultural and mineral commodities in the same markets is
high. This meets the preconditions for cartelisation which may offer
short-term income gains. It is questionable, though, whether national
authorities have a genuine interest to maintain cartel discipline and
whether they are prepared to sacrifice national gains for the sake of
sustaining a cartel policy. Concerning access to the markets for
manufactures in industrialised countries even regional groupings may
lack sufficient countervailing power to win concessions.

On the demand side, import demand could be pooled. However, a joint import policy may be even more difficult to achieve than supply coordination since countries mostly import heterogeneous manufactured goods, and import requirements of countries differ by income levels. Furthermore, integration schemes mostly remain small entities in terms of purchasing power even if they should succeed in bundling their import demand, e.g. through state trading. They will not be able to build up monopsonistic positions and enjoy income gains through imposing an optimum tariff or achieving terms of trade gains through other channels.

Politically, collective bargaining may offer gains in voting power in international negotiations. In addition, it may enable countries to shift parts of their defence expenditures to third countries if the latter ones view regional coherence as an element of their utility function. The same may hold true for access to foreign aid and other external resources. Donor countries may save costs if they negotiate with representatives of a region instead of many countries separately. Generally spoken, regionalism seems to have more appeal in the political than in the economic arena because it allows for producing international collective goods like regional security and because a cosmopolitan alternative to regionalism is mostly not available.

2. Consensus Building on Regional Political and Security Issues

RIDC may serve as a vehicle to commit neighbouring countries to common objectives if the direct way of political integration is not feasible. Such objectives are easier to identify if a common actual or perceived external political threat exists. The history of some regional groupings among developing countries bears witness to this argument, e.g. the Association of Southeast Asian Nations (ASEAN) or the Southern African Development Coordination Conference (SADCC). Consensus building about political objectives of common interest requires mutual consultations and may lead to regional regimes of norms and rules or even concrete agreements [Keohane, 1982; Krasner, 1982]. The benefits which such agreements promise comprise the receipt of mutual political support and burden sharing in security issues. Such benefits have to be paid for with restraints in national unilateral policy making and, possib-

ly, financial contributions to the joint purpose. As long as the balance
between restraints and benefits is positive, consensus building is profitable from the single country's point of view [cf. in detail Krasner,
1982; Hoffmann, 1983]. In other words, refraining from maximising the
self-interest of individual partners now is conditioned by the expectation
that other partners return this favour when needed in future [Jervis,
1982; Keohane, 1982].

It is important to note that such regional cooperation does not render the nation-state obsolete. On the contrary, it contributes to its
survival because cooperation strengthens the effectiveness of domestic
policy making. However, regional cooperation may come under pressure
when the external threat vanishes. Then, the relative attractiveness of
individual versus collective actions may change in the way that the
latter does not promise more rewarding results than the former [Hoff-
mann, 1983, p. 34].

3. Provision of a Scapegoat for Unpopular Policy Decisions

Regional integration both in the sense of trade and factor integration and project-specific cooperation constrains national policies, either
by requiring policy changes or by binding countries not to change existing policies. Such loss of national sovereignty may prove to be a gain
for individual countries as well as for national policymakers. To start
with the latter, public choice theory and the theory of political economy
suggest that policymakers are rationally acting agents which maximise
their individual benefits rather than those of the community. Giving up
national autonomy to some extent is equivalent to shifting the responsibility for certain policies to some relatively anonymous supranational
body which is more remote from the political clientele than national institutions. Under the objective of maintaining power it is rational to shift
so-called "dirty jobs" to the supranational body and to deny own responsibility. These "jobs" are policies which benefit relatively small
interest groups at the expense of the majority of voters such as sector-
specific tariffs and subsidies. A somewhat different viewpoint is presented by Pelkmans [1983; 1986] who argues that sector-specific policies
are important means to redistribute income and, hence, a major instru-

ment to influence the political clientele. National politicians will seek to keep such policies under their control and instead shift general economic policies such as tariff cuts across the board to regional institutions.

Both arguments have in common that policies which are profitable in terms of being applauded by identifiable voters and pressure groups and which can be attributed to policy makers will not be delegated to supra-national bodies. Costs arise, however, if such bodies expand their competence and consequently their demand for resources and if national governments lose control over them.

As far as the gain for individual countries is concerned, regional commitments may help to discipline the domestic political opposition against the removal of national price distortions. Yet, this may require an additional compensation of groups losing their subsidies. Gains for countries as well as for politicians may coincide, but do not necessarily do so.

C. Barriers to Integration

I. Natural Barriers

Barriers to RIDC have played an important role in assessing reasons for failures. Such barriers may be rooted in geographical conditions
and/or historical developments. They are frequently mentioned in the
context of low-income regional groupings in Sub-Saharan Africa. Natural
barriers have in common that they are constraints to integration outside
the responsibility of partner countries. If they are prohibitive, regional
integration is nondiscriminatory, that is noneffective (Iceland-New Zea-
land case). Barriers may not only arise from transportation costs, e. g.
Sub-Saharan surface transport, but also from communication costs. Unfor-
tunately, there is no information available on how such costs have
changed over time in RIDC and how they compare to effective rates of
protection. It seems plausible to assume that conditions of surface and
especially air transport have improved in Sub-Saharan Africa since the
late 1960s and early 1970s when they were extremely poor.[1] Lower
natural barriers to trade have exposed local industries to stronger competition from neighbouring countries. Increasing competitive pressure
could induce countries to stop intraregional trade liberalisation and even
to implement new tariffs as substitutes for natural barriers.

Different languages are a passepartout for cultural, legal, administrative and institutional barriers as the dichotomy between the anglophone and francophone West African countries suggests. As colonial
languages proved to be the instrument for nation-state building and were
used as a tool of governmental rule, governments were not prepared to
introduce vernacular languages spreading across borders or to accept
one common colonial language. Barriers caused by languages, however,
are not unsurmountable or prohibitive. They add to other barriers which
are more binding constraints as the Latin American or North African
experience underlines where RIDC did not suffer from language barriers.
If intraregional trade is mutually profitable the social invention of
agreeing to a common working language in commerce will soon be made
even if governments might subsidise the use of their language in diplo-

---

[1] Cf. Langhammer [1978, pp. 151-159] for estimates of transportation
costs in the Central African Customs and Economic Union (CACEU).

matic, scientific or political circles. The same will hold for standards and norms linked to languages.

The colonial heritage as another natural barrier is a catchword for sustained commercial and political links between the former metropolitan power and the newly founded states. Economically, it has again material- ised in Sub-Saharan Africa where the communication and transport net- work discriminated against intraregional trade. Furthermore, firms from metropolitan countries retained some monopoly power and could export manufactures to African countries at prices above those of competitors, either through tied aid, state trading or through exploiting nontariff barriers (NTBs) build up against other OECD countries [Kreinin, 1973; Ndongko, 1973]. To what extent such monopolies tend to impede intra- regional trade is difficult to measure since the elasticity of substitution between products originating from partner countries and from the metro- politan country can hardly be estimated empirically.[1] Over time, colonial ties are likely to have decreased in importance, perhaps more visibly in anglophone than in francophone countries which are still strongly linked to France through monetary cooperation (Franc Zone).

II. Political Barriers

The majority of developing countries is still in the process of find- ing national identity. Obviously, this process applies particularly to African and Asian countries which have aimed at neutralising problems of multiracial and multitribal societies through a common umbrella of a na- tion-state. Such a search for identity can constitute an obstacle to RIDC. Borders gain in importance as the inflow of goods, factors and ideas will probably be constrained in order to facilitate the finding of national identity. Under such conditions, neighbouring countries can become competing units and rivals for scarce internal and external re- sources. Nationalism may be spurred and border conflicts provoked. The history of manifold conflicts between developing countries even within integration schemes bears witness to the relevance of political barriers. They tend to be the stronger the less costly it appears to intervene into

---

[1] For a theoretical discussion of measuring elasticities of substitution, cf. Sawyer, Sprinkle [1989].

intraregional resource flows, i.e. the less important markets of neighbouring countries are for national economic welfare. In some cases the good performance of neighbouring countries will serve as a scapegoat for own failures as politicians tend to argue in terms of a zero-sum game.

Political barriers can also be built up if controversies on fundamental issues of the economic order exist. In many developing countries, an economic order has not been developed through experience, consensus or "tâtonnement", but was inherited from the colonial past or arbitrarily fixed by the political leaders of newly independent states. Two very different economic order systems within an integration scheme are prohibitive to consensus building as was shown in East Africa (Tanzania and Kenya) and to a lesser extent also in Latin America (Peru and Chile).

III. Economic Barriers

Even if natural and political barriers are not important a guarantee cannot be given for an efficient regional integration as there may be economic barriers against RIDC. One such barrier is the absolute level of income. For low-income countries static trade effects as well as dynamic production effects will be negligible given the low level of overall modern industrial activities [Brada, Mendez, 1983]. Another barrier are differences between partner countries concerning the income level. They will in the short run lead to some polarisation as synergy effects will work in favour of the relatively more advanced partner countries [Vaitsos, 1978]. Capital will accumulate in more advanced countries, and labour will tend to migrate. The markets of backward countries are so small that they can easily be supplied by industries of the advanced countries which have excess capacities and hence do not need new investment. Therefore, intraregional trade imbalances in manufactures may emerge very rapidly if industrial capacities are idle and if trade in agricultural products between the relatively resource-abundant backward countries and the relatively capital-abundant central states is not liberalised. Problems of trade imbalances will be exacerbated if no exchange rate adjustment of backward countries is possible because of their membership in a monetary union like in francophone West Africa and partly in Central Africa as well. It is important to note that trade imbalances do not indicate that a backward country is worse off compared to non-membership. The state may be better off but its performance may still lag behind that of the central state, and this matters politically.

Growing trade imbalances can aggravate the touchy issue of losses of government revenues in the netimporting backward countries. Such losses may either occur in the case of trade creation when ceteris paribus the tax base in the importing country shrinks as domestic production will be replaced by partner countries´ imports. Alternatively, the state incurs losses of customs revenues if trade is diverted from non-members to member countries. Given the weak tax base and the dependence of budget revenues on customs especially in low-income countries, growing trade imbalances will sooner or later provoke the resistance of netimporters against liberalising intraregional trade.

A further barrier is constituted by different perceptions of regional industrialisation planning. If decisions on investment in industries of regional importance are not made by markets but through intergovernmental negotiations, different cost-benefit analyses of alternative industries and industrial locations may prevent consensus.

IV. Politico-Economic Barriers

Economic barriers to RIDC have an additional dimension related to the economic rationale of policy formulation. Economic theory generally assumes that utility functions of governments and nations are identical and that politicians strive to increase the welfare of the population as a whole. The political economy of government decision making has shown, however, that governments may pursue objectives such as securing their own power and influence which are not necessarily in the best interest of the countries concerned. Similarly, politicians are believed to behave rationally in the sense that they maximise their own utility e. g. in terms of bending to the demands of their own electorate sometimes even at the expense of national welfare. Furthermore, governments and politicians may have a direct economic stake in public decision making as their own income and wealth can depend on these decisions to a substantial degree.

Governments and politicians will evaluate the membership in a regional grouping on the basis of their own net benefit. These may become negative if RIDC implies only marginal benefits but is achieved only at substantial costs in terms of political power or income foregone. Such a cost-benefit calculus may be able to explain why countries have left regional groupings and why mutually agreed policy decisions are not implemented in member countries. In the case of nonimplementation, governments may value membership highly because of associated benefits derived from common external activities (increased security, attraction of foreign aid), but they are not prepared to shoulder the costs of opening up their own markets.

D. Regional Integration Schemes in Operation

I. Synopsis of Institutional and Economic Developments

Despite substantial differences in historical roots (Section C. I) and integration philosophy all major integration schemes have aimed at economic integration by promoting intraregional trade (Synoptical Table 1). This target was pursued with varying degrees of ambition. Some schemes (Latin American Integration Association (LAIA), Preferential Trade Area for Eastern and Southern African States (PTA), ASEAN) focussed on preferential trading arrangements, while others (Central American Common Market (CACM), CACEU, West African Economic Community (WAEC)) intended to go all the way to a common market with a common external tariff and factor mobility. In addition, the Andean Pact had embarked upon regional industrialisation programmes to promote a more equitable regional development.

The achievements of RIDC varied across integration schemes and over time even more than the means employed (Synoptical Table 1). Promoting intraregional trade has not or not yet been successful in the Economic Community of West African States (ECOWAS), PTA and ASEAN. A second group of integration schemes recorded a promising start, but soon stagnated (LAIA) or even disintegrated again (CACM, Andean Pact). The relatively most successful schemes were those which could sustain the integration level inherited from the earlier colonial period (WAEC, CACEU).

Success or failure in RIDC has, however, not decisively influenced economic development of member countries of integration schemes. An outstanding example are the ASEAN countries which on average experienced rapid economic progress although regional integration remained minimal (Table 1). All in all, the pattern of economic development among integration schemes rather reflects the impact of external constraints and domestic policies. Furthermore, economic development became increasingly imbalanced between member countries of integration schemes as is shown by high coefficients of variation for major economic indicators (Table 1). Centrifugal forces have clearly dominated integration efforts. The reasons for these unfavourable developments are discussed in detail in the following sections.

Synoptical Table 1 – Targets, Means, and Achievements of Major Integration Schemes

	Targets	Means	Achievements
LAIA	Gradual and progressive establishment of an area of economic preferences with an equity-oriented three-tier category of more developed, intermediate and less developed members, no time schedule for targets to be achieved	Regional tariff preferences, additional bilateral preferences, industrial cooperation, clearing and credit schemes	In 1987, about 40 per cent of intra-LAIA imports came under items eligible for preferences (Table 2) with intercountry variations in product coverage. Tariff cuts in trade in specific industries between congenial partners (e.g. Argentina and and Brazil) are overproportionate
Andean Pact	Gradual formation of a customs union; regional industrialisation programmes; common investment policies	Tariff cuts, common minimum external tariff, joint industrial programming schemes	Serious delays and setbacks during the 1980s; trade liberalisation programme is rescheduled; joint industrialisation programmes failed
CACM	Customs union for goods originating in the member countries; removal of foreign exchange constraints in intratrade	Common external tariff, clearing house arrangement	The CACM after a convincing start in the 1960s disintegrated in the 1970s because of political and later on economic difficulties; revitalisation is underway but the late 1960s stage of integration has not yet been achieved
WAEC	Customs union for processed goods originating in the WAEC, compensation for customs revenues foregone. Full dismantling of internal tariff and NTBs to trade targetted for the early 1990s	Preference scheme replacing internal import duties on industrial goods by the "regional cooperation tax" which funds a compensation scheme	Relatively successful in terms of intraregional trade shares; intratrade in raw materials is widely exempt from customs duties; compensation scheme is effective, labour mobility is relatively high. The WAEC, however, is affected by the general economic malaise of West African economies and by growing disparities among member countries

Synoptical Table 1 continued

	Targets	Means	Achievements
ECOWAS	Gradual elimination of TBs and NTBs on intratrade in manufactured products over a period of 4 to 10 years, depending on categories of countries and products. Mutual trade in agricultural products and handicrafts is to be totally liberalised from the outset	Cooperation, compensation and development fund; technical and specialised commission for trade, customs, immigration, monetary and payments matters; for industry, agriculture and natural resources for transport, telecommunication and energy; and for social and cultural affairs	Trade liberalisation is still awaiting implementation. Expulsion of ECOWAS nationals by Nigeria in the mid-1980s jeopardised efforts towards free movement of labour
CACEU	Customs union, free mobility of labour	"Single tax" as substitute for customs duties on intratrade; common investment code; common external tariff, solidarity fund	Decline in the intensity of integration compared to the 1960s and early 1970s, intratrade is low; no progress in labour mobility; CACEU is outcompeted by a community which includes Zaire
PTA	Reduction and eventual elimination of TBs and NTBs on intratrade, removal, ease of restrictions in transit trade; removal of foreign exchange constraints in intratrade	Three-tier preference scheme for originating products, clearing house facilities, liability insurance scheme for transit trade	Major parts of the liberalisation programme are not yet implemented, clearing house still lacks attractiveness, PTA of potential interest for few core countries only
ASEAN	Preferencial trade area; joint industrialisation in specific manufacturing sub-sectors in regional joint ventures; improved bargaining power concerning access to OECD markets	Preferential trading arrangement for selected items, ASEAN Industrial Projects Scheme (AIP), ASEAN Industrial Complementation Scheme (AIC), ASEAN Industrial Joint Ventures (AIJV), permanent institutionalised dialogue with OECD countries	Preferential trading arrangement has had little impact on intra-ASEAN trade; AIPs and AICs failed and AIJVs are still to be implemented; dialogue with OECD countries is successful; cohesion towards third countries and good individual economic performance puts modest progress of integration into the shade; cooperation increasingly dominates over integration

Source: UNCTAD [b; c; d]; general literature cited in the bibliography.

Table 1 - Basic Economic Indicators and Measures of Dispersion of Major
          Integration Schemes

	(1)	(2)	(3)	(4)	(5)	(6)	(7)	(8)
LAIA	358.4	1890	2.5(a)	684420	6.7(b)	1.8(b)	5.3(c)	4.4(c)
CV(d)	1.30	0.46	1.18	1.42	0.47	2.15	1.25	1.19
Andean								
Pact	84.6	1650	1.1(a)	141780	4.6(b)	1.2(b)	-2.7(c)	2.0(c)
CV(d)	0.53	0.67	2.37	0.71	0.39	2.51	3.60	1.81
CACM	24.1	960	-0.7(a)	22830	5.0(b)	0(b)	4.1(c)	-0.2(c)
CV(d)	0.46	0.33	16.2	0.33	0.30	3.32	0.51	-3.42
WAEC	47.2	400	0.4(a)	20550	3.9(b)	2.4(b)	5.8(c)	3.8(c)
CV(d)	0.44	0.52	7.32	0.82	0.71	0.96	0.60	1.30
ECOWAS	185.2	370	0.6(a)	53140	5.0(b)	1.5(b)	8.0(c)	-1.5(c)
CV(d)	2.21	0.46	14.8	1.50	0.59	1.82	0.98	4.67
CACEU(e)	22.0	770	1.8(a)	20300(e)	3.5(b)	3.3(b)	5.3(c)	4.4(c)
CV(d)	1.07	1.08	2.11	1.21	0.76	0.66	0.85	1.56
PTA(f)	151.8	270	0.2(a)	33640	4.0(b)	2.2(b)	1.5(c)	1.3(c)
CV(d)	1.20	0.83	2.0	0.7	0.43	0.67	2.10	6.82
ASEAN(g)	302.5	690	3.9(a)	203580	7.6(b)	3.7(b)	6.5(c)	6.3(c)
CV(d)	1.10	1.37	0.46	0.47	0.20	0.67	0.39	0.80

(1) = Population 1987 in mill.
(2) = Gross National Product (GNP) per capita 1987 in US $
(3) = Average annual growth of GNP per capita 1965-1987
(4) = Gross Domestic Product (GDP) 1987 in mill. US $
(5) = Average annual growth of GDP 1965-1980
(6) = Average annual growth of GDP 1980-1987
(7) = Growth of merchandise exports 1965-1980
(8) = Growth of merchandise exports 1980-1987

(a) Regional average weighted with the population of member countries
1987. - (b) Regional average weighted with the 1987 GDP of member
countries. - (c) Regional average weighted with 1987 merchandise exports of member countries. - (d) Coefficient of variation: standard
deviation/average of indicators for individual member countries. -
(e) Excluding Equatorial Guinea. - (f) For indicators (4)-(8) excluding Comoros, Djibouti, and Swaziland. - (g) Excluding Brunei.

Source: World Bank [1989b]; own calculations.

II. Regional Integration in Latin America

1. The Latin American Free Trade Association

The foundation of the Latin American Free Trade Association (LAFTA/ ALALC) by Argentina, Brazil, Chile, Mexico, Paraguay, Peru, and Uruguay in 1960[1] was the outcome of two different perceptions. On the one hand, the so-called "cepalismo" view fostered by the Economic Commission for Latin America (ECLA) gave strong support to regional import substitution as a countervailing strategy against deteriorating terms of trade and dependence on imports of capital goods from indus-trialised countries. On the other hand, vested interests of the large member countries urged for new markets for local inward-oriented indus-tries which were not competitive on world markets. Regional preferences were looked upon as an easy way towards expanding the market frontiers without bearing the costs of adjusting to world market conditions.

In comparison, the second perception proved to be the dominant one. This paved the way to distributional conflicts when it became evi-dent that the benefits from gaining access to markets of neighbouring countries were unequally distributed given the different stages of indus-trialisation within LAFTA. The smaller countries did not prove as buoy-ant absorbers of LAFTA-originating products as were expected by the net exporters. Consequently, the latter ones did not offer compensation schemes which would have been one possibility to settle disputes over unbalanced regional trade. As a result, the time schedule for the com-pletion of a free trade area soon became obsolete.

Initially, LAFTA members had agreed upon a twelve year transition period during which the mutual trade barriers were to be dismantled following item-by-item negotiations in a two-tier approach. So-called common lists of items eligible for preferential treatment were expected to be accepted by all members for all members. In addition, each member was requested to offer national lists of products for which tariffs were to be reduced by at least 8 per cent after each negotiation round. Some compensation or transfer elements were introduced through options for

---

[1] Colombia and Ecuador became members in 1961, Venezuela in 1966 and Bolivia in 1967.

member countries to confine preferences to the backward partners within LAFTA but such preferences did not play a role as no clear-cut defini- tion on indicators of "backwardness" was agreed upon.

LAFTA in operation failed to achieve all major objectives. Items on the common list were never fully liberalised and national lists remained unimportant until they were given up with the foundation of the Andean Group in 1969. In deviation from the initial focus on trade integration, industrial cooperation on a bilateral level was initiated from the very beginning, but it was not until the apparent failure of the free-trade objective at the end of the 1960s that industrial cooperation moved into the centre of Latin American integration. It was intended to give an impulse to industrial policy coordination and to spur the production of more sophisticated goods not yet traded within LAFTA. Again, as in trade, bilateral agreements in few sectors were mostly confined to the Big Three (Argentina, Brazil, and Mexico) where multinational enter- prises could organise intraindustry specialisation across borders [Balassa, 1979].

Compared to other integration schemes, especially the CACM and the East African Community (EAC), there is little empirical evidence available on the effects of LAFTA, probably because of the apparent failure of the pure trade integration approach pursued by LAFTA. One hint can be taken from the development of the share of intra-LAFTA trade in total trade of LAFTA during the early stage of this scheme. Intra-LAFTA trade shares climbed from 8 per cent in 1960 to 10 per cent in 1970 and even to 13 per cent in 1980 [UNCTAD, a]. But what emer- ges as a success is simply the outcome of rising world market prices of commodities which would have been traded anyway without tariff prefer- ences. Trade in commodities (for instance, wheat from Argentina, coffee from Colombia and Brazil, meat and rice from Uruguay, crude oil from Venezuela and Mexico, and copper from Peru and Chile) grew faster than trade in goods subject to LAFTA tariff preferences (so-called negotiated products). Until the mid-1980s the share of negotiated products in intra- regional imports of members under the new LAIA preference scheme has remained low (40 per cent of total intraregional imports in 1986; Table 2). In addition, there were large differences between the advanced countries (the Big Three) on the one hand, importing up to 58 per cent of LAIA-originating products under preferential agreements, and the

Table 2 - Intra-LAIA Trade, 1985-1988

	Exports				Imports					
	1985	1986	1987	1988(a)	1985		1986		1987	1988(a)
	mill. US $					per cent(b)	mill. US $	per cent(b)	mill. US $	
					Intra-LAIA Trade					
Argentina	1485	1557	1314	1570	1299	45.2	1597	55.5	1725	2058
Bolivia	403	412	328	300	308	1.9	257	.	334	361
Brazil	2231	2879	3027	3696	1712	41.8	1939	58.2	1896	1874
Colombia	288	400	574	480	882	18.8	654	24.0	652	735
Chile	534	666	837	878	784	32.9	732	32.9	950	1451
Ecuador	132	150	174	469	417	11.0	310	14.2	542	567
Mexico	597	635	803	864	565(c)	32.0	351(c)	46.4	291	462
Paraguay	97	152	158	204	273	4.4	268	1.5	265	246
Peru	349	365(a)	351	371	442	45.0	596	37.8	726	764
Uruguay	238	426	364	330	197	38.6	350	41.1	564	587
Venezuela	715	379	617	584	654	9.5	620	11.9	805	935
Total	7069	8021	8547	9746	7533	30.1	7674	40.0	8750	10040
					Extra-LAIA Trade					
Argentina	6911	5295	5046	6864	2515		3127		4093	3482
Bolivia	270	228	242	220	383		416		432	421
Brazil	23408	19503	23202	29704	12619		13618		14684	14126
Colombia	3264	4708	4450	4870	3249		3198		3576	3435
Chile	3230	3386	4161	5594	1959		2182		2843	3156
Ecuador	2773	2036	1843	1691	1391		1496		1506	1508
Mexico	21269	15140	19729	20726	12895(c)		11158(c)		12470	18038
Paraguay	207	81	195	249	229		310		330	274
Peru	2546	2145(a)	1852	2405	1325		1795		2277	1925
Uruguay	615	672	842	990	422		327		591	493
Venezuela	15308	8234	9934	9146	6650		7047		7906	8015
Total	79801	61428	71496	82459	43637		44674		50708	54873

(a) Estimates. - (b) Of which eligible for preferences (negotiated imports). - (c) Fob value.

Source: ALADI [b, 1988, Nr. 1,5 und 6, 1989, Nr. 1].

backward partners like Paraguay and Bolivia on the other hand which imported but a very small share of goods from partner countries under preferential conditions. As a result, more telling than the intraregional trade share of about 15 per cent in 1988 is the fact that in 1986 nego-tiated imports comprised no more than 5.9 per cent of total LAIA im-ports.

Analytically, the question of trade diversion versus trade creation within LAFTA deserves more attention than the development of intraregional trade shares. Results differ by approaches applied, but there is evidence for more trade diversion than trade creation (Synoptical Table A1). For instance, George et al. [1977] estimated import demand functions for each LAFTA country by imports from member and nonmember countries. They found LAFTA to account for a cumulative increase in intraregional trade of US $ 2.6 bill. while diverting imports worth US $ 3.9 bill. from nonmember countries. Thus, there was a clear preponderance of trade diversion and even a net trade diverting effect, i.e. a decrease of total trade in absolute terms (calculated as the difference between both changes). More recent research applying a shift-share analysis for manufactured imports of the Big Three in the 1962/63-1978/79 period strongly supports the hypothesis of trade diversion as the major source of growth of intra-LAFTA trade [Langhammer, Spinanger, 1984, pp. 56-63].

What is common to all studies is the conclusion that the pure trade integration process of LAFTA failed to decentralise trade flows in processed goods across all member countries and to produce a "training ground" effect for exporting outside the region as was expected by some politicians and scholars [e.g. Balassa, 1973, p. 180]. This is confirmed by empirical analyses provided in Table A1.

2. The Latin American Integration Association

The failure of LAFTA induced Latin American politicians to choose a new approach of loose cooperation providing scope for differentiated approaches to intraregional trade liberalisation on a bilateral level. This strategy mix of cooperation and integration became institutionalised with the foundation of the Latin American Integration Association (LAIA/ALADI) in 1980. Neither a free trade area nor a uniform regional preference margin applying to all members across the board was aimed at but bilateral tariff preferences and regional tariff preferences in some items for all members. The new concept of LAIA is that of consolidating and promoting the existing bilateral trade relations instead of subsidising new import-substitution industries through preferential treatment as it was intended by LAFTA. This implies a sizeable increase in the variance of both preferential trade and access conditions among partner countries. By 1987, regional preference margins ranged between 4 per cent for exports of the Big Three to the three smaller partners Bolivia, Ecuador and Paraguay and 22 per cent for imports of the Big Three from the countries. As overvalued exchange rates have often rendered tariff protection ineffective in Latin American countries [e.g. in Argentina, cf. Wogart, Marques, 1985], there was not much trade expansion to be expected from preferential tariffs.

The ongoing internal process of differentiation was further accentuated by external challenges relevant for member countries to different degrees (oil price shock, debt problem) and corresponding internal responses. In total, efficiency losses of discriminatory trade policies are likely to be lower in the looser type of LAIA integration than in the rigid LAFTA type.

Given the severe foreign exchange bottlenecks of the highly indebted Latin American countries, the issue of saving foreign exchange through reciprocal clearing arrangements has received much attention in LAIA. The LAIA Payments System allows for invoicing intraregional trade in local currencies and to confine payments in convertible foreign currency to clearing balances and advance transfers. After two decades of Payments and Credit Arrangements in operation it has been achieved to reduce the share of foreign currency transfers in total operations channelled through the arrangements from 30 per cent in 1966 to 24 per cent in 1988 (Table A2). Far-reaching expectations with regard to foreign exchange savings and the reduction of transaction costs had, however, to be discounted. Neither were savings high in terms of total financial transactions nor could the arrangements offset trade-policy-induced impediments to intraregional trade expansion such as the lacking dismantling of NTBs [Fischer, 1983]. Approaches within LAIA to stimulate barter trade and compensation arrangements in order to save foreign exchange [Hodara, 1985] support the view that clearing arrangements have failed to ease the foreign exchange constraints. In addition, the emergence of the debt crisis and the subsequent liquidity constraints in the mid-1980s led to an extensive use of the regular lines of credits and to a rapid exhaustion of the credit ceilings. As a result, some member countries had to clear their debits with each other before the lapse of the normal 120-day settlement period [UNCTAD, c].

Viewed against the objective to expand intraregional trade, LAIA has not performed better than LAFTA as can be seen from the low progress in raising the share of items eligible for preferential treatment [Langhammer, Spinanger, 1984, Table A18; ALADI, a]. Nor can it be concluded that LAIA has fulfilled the function of a training ground for gaining extraregional competitiveness better than LAFTA. What can be said is that in the past LAIA has proved to be a less costly way to regionalisation than LAFTA. Should, however, a new programme of regional import substitution be put in place on the basis of national lists of goods imported from third countries and with preference margins raised substantially – as it had been designed for the end of the 1980s [UNCTAD, b, p. 14] – costs would increase again.

3. The Andean Pact

The development of the subgroup within LAFTA/LAIA, the Andean Pact, mirrors three things: the initial fear of smaller countries to be overridden by the Big Three, the euphoria of finding an alternative – more "development-oriented" – approach to integration, and finally, the disillusions resulting from distributive conflicts which broke out even within a more homogeneous group of countries than LAFTA was.

The smaller Latin American countries frustrated by the shortcomings of LAFTA perceived two essentials as guidelines for their genuine approach to integration: (a) more outward orientation in the regional context than those LAFTA members with a large internal market, and (b) more elements of planning in the regional industrialisation process in order to take account of equity considerations. Accordingly, the foundation act, the Cartagena Agreement of 1969 negotiated by Bolivia, Chile, Colombia, Ecuador, and Peru (Venezuela followed in 1973) included trade integration cum "regionally balanced" industrialisation. The former was envisaged through the formation of a free trade area and later on a customs union with a common external tariff, whereas the latter target was to be achieved by regional investment plans (so-called Sectorial Programs of Industrial Development) and by harmonisation of domestic policies [Heldt, 1972]. A common treatment of foreign investment (Decision 24) which included restrictive practices such as an indigenisation requirement, limits to profit remittances, and monopolies for national firms in some sectors marked the beginning of domestic policy coordination on a regional level.

Both instruments of integration, the common external tariff and regional industrialisation programmes were bound to fail when they conflicted with national development plans. Ultimately, they would have meant a subordination and finally surrender of national sovereignty which the countries were not willing to endorse. Fundamental disagreements on principles of the economic order such as between Peru and Chile in the mid-1970s - to mention an extreme case - which led to the withdrawal of Chile from the Andean Pact in 1976, were only the peak of the iceberg. Even more congenial countries in the Andean Group pursued entirely different economic policies and were unprepared to bear the economic and political costs of policy coordination.

Economically, a common external tariff would have resulted in considerable trade diversion as the initial level of intraregional trade was low. When the decisions were to be implemented, homogeneity among member countries proved to be a chimera. The industrially more advanced member country Colombia strove for a relatively low level of external protection in order not to penalise its manufactured exports and to avoid a real appreciation of its currency. On the other hand, Venezuela tried to cope with the negative consequences of the Dutch disease effect for the competitiveness of its non-petroleum sectors against imports and urged for a high external tariff. [1]

Regional industrialisation by means of attributing specific industries to specific countries through administrative procedures faced high costs too. Inefficiencies due to planning which became already visible on the national level grew substantially when the regional level was involved. A sacrifice to efficiency criteria for the sake of an equitable distribution of net benefits could have theoretically been lowered by multinational ownership from all members but this would have meant the transfer of vested interests from the state to the firm level. Factor mobility which could have eased the problems inherent in regional industrialisation was never allowed within the Andean Pact. Furthermore, under regional in-

---

[1] For a lucid summary, cf. Blejer [1986, pp. 20-24].

dustrialisation employment foregone would have been sizeable in countries supplying the regional market under high protection since larger production runs would have fostered capital-intensive techniques. Thus, the trend observed in Colombia that intraregional manufactured exports were much more capital-intensive than extraregional ones would have been enhanced [Wogart, 1978, p. 111 f.].

Politically, surrendering national sovereignty proved to be inconsistent with ambitious national development programmes and assessments of national benefits from integration. The result was that (after a number of internal crises caused by the halt of industrial programming and the nonimplementation of the common external tariff) conflicts culminated in 1983 when trade among Andean Pact member states broke down. Since that time a substantial revision of the Cartagena provisions is under way. The so-called Quito Protocol of 1987 has set new positions. Similar to LAIA, new plans are less ambitious and give more scope for discretion and flexibility. According to the Protocol, the treatment of foreign investment is going to be liberalised and cooperation targets in science and technology have replaced objectives of domestic policy coordination. The sectoral development programming now aims at raising the efficiency of existing programmes (metal, chemical, petrochemical and steel industries) instead of extending it to new sectors. The bold project of a common automobile industry has been as abandoned as the objective of a full-scale common external tariff. In total, the Andean Pact approaches LAIA, still with more focus on industrial and agricultural cooperation but at a much more modest profile.

4. The Central American Common Market

The Central American Common Market (CACM/MCCA) founded in December 1960 by Guatemala, Honduras, El Salvador, Nicaragua and later on joined by Costa Rica (1962) belongs to those integration groupings the trade effects of which have been extensively scrutinised by many scholars.[1] This interest can be explained by the relatively compact na-

---

[1] E.g. Aitken, Lowry [1973]; Nugent [1974]; Segal [1967]; Wilford [1970]; Willmore [1972; 1974; 1976; 1979]; Wionczek [1972].

ture of the grouping comprising small countries, its straightforward approach assisted by a relatively high degree of homogeneity and a large amount of intraregional trade as well as by its performance during the 1961-1969 period. After this period interest came to a rapid standstill due to the emerging disintegration tendencies.

Measured in terms of integration instruments applied, the CACM followed the most far-reaching approach of all groupings. It aimed at liberalising intraregional trade fully parallel to the introduction of a common external tariff, envisaged the introduction of region-wide monopolistic industries to be allocated equally among the five members [Ramsett, 1969], implemented special promotion schemes for new import-substituting industries, designed the harmonisation of fiscal incentives for investment, launched a Central Bank for Economic Integration as a multilateral financing facility, and finally, introduced clearing facilities and institutions for compensation.

During the first decade success in trade liberalisation was doubt-less by far larger than in regional industrial programming. With respect to the latter, protocols specifying the status of regional industries for tyres produced in Guatemala as well as for soda ash and insecticides produced in Nicaragua were ratified and implemented but with large delays. Ultimately, they were jeopardised by parallel investments in other member countries (tyres in Costa Rica). Thus, trade integration remained the nucleus of the CACM. By 1970, the stage of a customs union was reached with very few exceptions. Intraregional trade shares climbed from 6 per cent in 1960 for imports and 7 per cent for exports to 24 and 27 per cent respectively, in 1970 [Heldt, 1974, Table 1]. Some products which were traded more intensively within the region also suc-ceeded to penetrate world markets, however, only until 1968. This pro-vides some support for RIDC as a training ground for exporters (Table A1).

Assessments on whether trade expansion within the CACM was of a trade-creating or trade-diverting type did not arrive at conclusive re-sults (Synoptical Table A1). However, when trade diversion occurred there was no doubt who had to bear the costs. It was Honduras and to a lesser extent Nicaragua while El Salvador and Guatemala were among those who gained. Between 1960 and 1968 El Salvador, for instance, more than quadrupled the share of manufactures in its annual exports to 27 per cent, and almost all manufactures were exported to CACM countries [SIECA, 1971].

Growing inequalities in bilateral trade balances were one reason for the gradual decline of the CACM, but not the only one. By the end of the 1960s all member countries incurred considerable losses in foreign exchange because of falling world market prices for coffee, bananas and cotton. In addition, the military conflict between Honduras and El Salvador in mid-1969 did not only put a break on the bilateral relations but also blocked intraregional transport and impeded trade flows heavily. Since that time sporadic approaches to revitalise the CACM have been undertaken but they were often impeded by either political conflicts and/or external economic shocks such as the oil price hikes and the debt problems. NTBs were introduced, exchange controls tightened, and clearing and payments mechanisms blocked. Over more than a decade, the CACM remained dormant and it was not until the mid-1980s that the existing institutional framework was used again in order to speak with one voice in external economic relations (an economic cooperation agreement with the EC was launched in 1987) and to put a new common external tariff into place. This tariff, however, is only part of total NTBs and tariff barriers (TBs) albeit one part which has become more important in recent years as the majority of CACM members devaluated in real terms and thus made tariffs effective again. The intraregional trade share has approached the 20 per cent level (Table A3) but this overall number hides much larger variances between the members than in the past (Table 3). The trend towards bilateralism is visible within CACM, too, and so is the new focus on cooperation in hardware (e.g. electricity grid) and software (trade information system, business meetings). Operational solutions for unsettled clearing balances are discussed (e.g. creation of so-called Central American Import Rights as payments units in intraregional trade) as long as the old clearing house arrangements - suspended in 1984 - are not yet in force.

To sum up major experiences gained from the CACM, the distributional conflicts were eminent even within this rather small number of relatively homogeneous countries. Regional import substitution prevailed and though it may have had some reallocation effects among the member countries, these effects must have remained small. The question whether the CACM could have survived without the military conflicts is obsolete.

Table 3 - Intraregional Exports in the CACM, 1960-1987

	1960	1968	1970	1973	1976	1980	1983	1986	1987(a)
Value (mill. US $)									
Guatemala	7.3	77.5	106.4	137.6	189.1	403.7	308.2	192.0	230.6
El Salvador	12.7	84.9	75.0	106.8	176.0	295.8	168.1	86.7	117.2
Honduras	7.4	31.3	19.1	13.3	37.7	83.9	61.4	18.8	25.0
Nicaragua	3.4	26.9	49.9	61.5	119.1	75.4	33.0	15.2	14.4
Costa Rica	1.9	37.7	48.7	69.2	134.9	270.3	187.1	100.5	104.7
CACM	32.7	258.3	299.1	388.2	656.8	1129.2	757.7	413.3	491.9
Structure (per cent)									
Guatemala	22.4	30.0	35.6	35.4	28.8	35.8	40.7	46.5	46.9
El Salvador	38.8	32.9	25.1	27.5	26.8	26.2	22.2	21.0	23.8
Honduras	22.6	12.1	6.4	3.4	5.8	7.4	8.1	4.5	5.1
Nicaragua	10.4	10.4	16.7	15.9	18.1	6.7	4.4	3.7	2.9
Costa Rica	5.8	14.6	16.3	17.8	20.5	23.9	24.7	24.3	21.3
CACM	100.0	100.0	100.0	100.0	100.0	100.0	100.0	100.0	100.0

(a) Preliminary.

Source: World Bank [1989a].

Doubtless, economic interdependences were too fragile even at the height of the "good" years to make a politically-rooted interference costly in economic terms. The fact that the CACM members never solved the issue of free migration within the region supports the view that factor mobility is an essential ingredient of growing economic interdependence.

5. The Caribbean Community

The Caribbean Community (CARICOM) was founded in 1973 as the successor of the Caribbean Free Trade Association (CARIFTA). It comprises thirteen mostly island states (Antigua and Barbuda, Bahamas, Barbados, Belize, Dominica, Grenada, Guyana, Jamaica, Montserrat, St. Kitts-Nevis, St. Lucia, St. Vincent, and Trinidad and Tobago). Four members (Barbados, Guyana, Jamaica, and Trinidad and Tobago) are institutionally acknowledged as the more advanced countries. Legally, the member countries have agreed upon a common external tariff. About 90 per cent of total intraregional trade has been freed from restrictions, but as CARICOM differentiates between more and less advanced member countries, only the former group has fully dismantled TBs against imports from the latter ones. All members are oriented towards trade with nonmember countries so that intraregional trade shares never exceeded low levels of 6 per cent for imports (1985) and 6-8 per cent for exports depending on commodity prices [Andic et al. 1971; UNCTAD, b]. Food products and other semi-processed goods dominate intraregional trade though preference margins in consumer goods were sizeable given relatively high tariff rates and an escalating tariff structure. For instance, effective rates of protection in the manufacturing sector of Jamaica in 1978 were estimated as 68 per cent for import-substituting sectors, 19 per cent for exports to CARICOM countries and -10 per cent for exports to the rest of the world [Foders, 1987, p. 78].

Basically, CARICOM is a customs union aiming at a common market which is institutionally designed in an appendix to the CARICOM Treaty. Rights of establishment, free trade in services and an industrial programming scheme are envisaged as steps towards a common market, but as many other instruments they have not yet been fully implemented. Rules of origin and the exploitation of marine resources are controversial issues not yet settled. The Caribbean Multilateral Clearing Facility reached its credit ceilings and ceased operations in 1984. A Caribbean Export Bank was launched in support of intraregional trade in nontraditional manufactured goods but it is not likely to offset trends to focus on trade with extraregional partners. The US, for instance, the most important trading partner of the CARICOM countries started the Caribbean Basin Initiative - among other things - in order to promote manufactured exports of CARICOM countries to the US. After two decades of experiences with integration, the CARICOM countries seem to be a prototype for regional cooperation, e.g. in common infrastructure projects and coordination of exploitation of natural resources, rather than a promising candidate for trade integration.

III. Regional Integration in Sub-Saharan Africa

1. Current Conditions for Integration in Sub-Saharan Africa

Sub-Saharan Africa provides the richest source of experiences with integration and cooperation schemes in the developing world. These experiences are full of dichotomies and ambivalence. There is obviously no African politician who has not taken a positive stance towards integration and cooperation starting from modest neighbourhood relations and ending with the all-embracing Lagos Plan of Action launched by the Organisation of African Unity (OAU) in April 1980 envisaging free trade among all African countries by the year 2000. But at the same time, the continent hosts the largest number of ineffective, failed or dormant groupings consisting of a secretariat and some adopted but not implemented plans. Both history and current state of the groupings mirror the extraordinary vulnerability and fragility of basic economic conditions in Sub-Saharan Africa. Between 1981 and 1986 intraregional trade in major African integration schemes declined both in current US dollar and as shares of total trade (Table A3).

Historically, there are three roots of integration. Firstly, those groupings which gained importance beyond narrow sub-regional circles are remnants of large colonial entities. For instance, in francophone Africa the two Federations of French West and Equatorial Africa were the predecessors of two customs unions. One was the Customs Union of West African States (CUWAS) which in 1973 became the WAEC when the former UN trusteeship territory Togo was admitted as a member. The other one was the Equatorial Customs Union (ECU) which together with Cameroon became the CACEU in 1964. Similarly, in anglophone East Africa the basis for integrating Kenya and Uganda with the mandated territory Tanganyika to a customs union was achieved in the colonial period, and the ill-fated East African Community (EAC), founded in 1967, basically strove for sustaining this level of integration while achieving an "equal" distribution of net benefits.

Secondly, new groupings were founded after gaining independence which either bridged the borderline between adjacent countries belonging to different colonial powers in the past but sharing some common elements such as the language (e.g. the Communities of the Great Lakes and of Central African States bringing the former Belgian colonies in contact with the French-originating countries). Alternatively, in West Africa the foundation of the ECOWAS in 1975 paid tribute to the fact that the anglophone "islands" (Ghana, Sierra Leone, Liberia and the politically powerful Nigeria) and the lusophone Guinea-Bissau maintained strong traditional commercial links with their francophone neighbours. This happened either through border trade or through large-scale smuggling with the francophone countries; through currency substitution with stable currencies like the Franc of the Communaute Financière Africaine (CFA) replacing the anglophone currencies; or through intensive labour migration.

Thirdly, new integration initiatives emerged in Southern Africa from the political conflict with South Africa and aimed at loosening the commercial ties to South Africa.

Economically, the current malaise of Sub-Saharan Africa has put integration efforts under considerable pressure because imports of goods and labour from member countries became restricted as a seemingly easy way to cope with balance of payments problems and unemployment. Yet, regardless of this malaise, there was one basic .dichotomy integration and cooperation in Sub-Saharan Africa has faced from the time when the countries became independent. That is the trade-off between the economic desirability of overcoming "balcanisation" and the political costs in terms of power erosion to the detriment of leaders in backward member countries. All leaders actively interfere into the economy of their countries and worry about their tax and rent base which is assumed to shrink in the integration process. In this respect, the claim for "equal distribution of benefits" basically appears to be a catchword for rent-conservation in backward member countries.

Given the myriad of integration efforts including project-linked cooperation (e.g. river basin organisations, regional organisations intended to fight pests and droughts), the following outline of major schemes in Sub-Saharan Africa can by no means be exhaustive. It aims at discussing the economic effects of integration tools implemented. Recent problems and decisions taken at summit meetings in the major groupings are summarised in Synoptical Table A2.

2. The West African Economic Community

The West African Economic Community (WAEC/CEAO) comprising Ivory Coast, Mali, Mauritania, Niger, Burkina Faso, and Senegal (Benin and Togo have a permanent observer status) was founded in 1974 to cope with the shortcomings of its predecessor, the CUWAS. Such short-comings were mainly identified as lacking compensation for trade diversion-induced losses in budget revenues [Robson, 1983, Chapter 4]. They emerged as a nonnegligible problem because of four peculiarities of the WAEC which in principle are conducive to intensive intraregional trade.

Firstly, the WAEC members are complementary in their production structures. Intersectoral division of labour is important in trade between Mali and Burkina Faso on the one hand as potential exporters of agricul-tural products, and Senegal and Ivory Coast on the other hand as rela-tively industrialised countries. The share of intraregional trade in total trade of the grouping amounted to 7 per cent in 1985 which is above the level achieved by other Sub-Saharan African groupings, e.g. the similar one in Central Africa [UNCTAD, a]. More illustrative than this overall figure is the fact that in 1981 as well as 1985 about 37-38 per cent of Ivorian manufactured exports and about 10 per cent of its total exports were directed to WAEC countries with some manufactured goods such as cement, fertilisers, household equipment and trailers exceeding the 70 per cent level (Table 4). However, only very few manufactured imports of the Ivory Coast originated from member countries. Such a regional distribution of intraregional trade suggests two things: a keen interest of the Ivorian industry in the regional market facilitating perhaps com-pensation schemes, and a concern of backward members´ industries to be outcompeted by suppliers from Senegal and Ivory Coast. In fact, indus-tries like footwear and textiles ranked highly as sensitive industries in intraregional trade liberalisation as they are produced in almost all member states.

Secondly, natural barriers to trade like prohibitive transportation costs are lower than elsewhere in Sub-Saharan Africa. Railway links exist between Senegal and Mali as well as between Ivory Coast and Bur-kina Faso. Policy-induced barriers to trade hence gain more attention in decision making of politicians in the less advanced member states who

Table 4 – Share of Intra-WAEC Imports and Exports of the Ivory Coast in Total Trade with Selected Products, 1981 and 1985 (per cent)

	SITC Rev. 2	1981	1985	Country of origin/ destination
		Imports		
Fertilizers, manufactured	562	1.3	17.2	Senegal
Pesticides	591	-	10.7	Senegal
Leather	611	-	52.0	Senegal
Rubber tyres, tubes	625	7.9	5.4	Senegal, Burkina Faso
Paper, precut	642	12.5	10.7	Senegal
Cotton fabrics	652	18.0	34.3	Senegal, Mali, Niger, Burkina Faso
Woven man-made fibre fabrics	653	5.3	7.5	Senegal
Textile fabrics, n.e.s.	658	7.1	9.4	Senegal
Metal household equipment	697	3.8	4.1	Senegal, Burkina Faso
Electrical machinery, n.e.s.	778	-	1.2	Senegal
Lorries	782.1	1.3	-	Senegal
Boats	793.2	-	6.3	Senegal
Footwear	851	4.1	4.2	Senegal
Printed matter	892	0.4	0.8	Senegal
Total manufactures	5-8-(67+68)	1.9	2.6	
Other products				
Fish	034.1	39.3	25.8	Senegal, Mauritania
Cigarettes	122.1	10.4	20.3	Senegal
Salt	278.3	87.9	89.4	Senegal
Total Trade		2.3	2.8	
		Exports		
Soap, cleansing	554	48.6	33.7	Burkina Faso,Mali,Niger
Fertilizers, manufactured	562	90.1	99.8	Burkina Faso, Mali
Polymerisation products	583	56.6	39.6	Burkina Faso, Mali
Pesticides	591	59.3	60.7	Mali, Burkina Faso
Veneers	634	18.3	12.2	Senegal, Mauritania
Textile yarn	651	57.1	45.2	Mali, Benin
Cotton fabrics	652	59.7	30.1	Mali, Senegal
Woven man-made fibre fabrics	653	72.0	65.1	Mali, Mauritania
Cement	661.2	95.4	97.0	Burkina Faso, Mali
Metal household equipment	697	56.4	74.4	Burkina Faso
Trailers	786	53.2	71.8	Burkina Faso, Mali
Footwear	851	22.6	34.2	Mali, Niger
Total manufactures	5-8-(67+68)	38.8	37.3	
Total Trade		10.0	9.5	

Source: UN [1982; 1987]; own calculations.

mostly have vested interests in protecting domestic industrialisation, no matter how inefficient these industries are.

Thirdly, the WAEC enjoys a high degree of factor mobility. The monetary union with a common central bank allows for free mobility of capital, and labour mobility is high as well. Though in the past initiatives to grant citizenship failed in the Ivory Coast there is a large amount of migration between landlocked and coastal member states. The effects of factor mobility on trade are ambivalent. The existence of the monetary union denies autonomous exchange rate changes (depreciation) to landlocked countries as a device to improve their competitive position vis-à-vis the more advanced coastal countries. Fiscal and wage policies are likely to be overburdened to substitute for lacking exchange rate adjustment within the union. Furthermore, theoretically labour mobility leading to migration from landlocked to coastal countries may have a wage-dumping effect in the coastal countries and impede the competitiveness of labour-intensive products in labour-abundant backward member states. Yet, on the other hand, factor mobility in general will tend to lower costs of information and transaction in intraregional trade and thus stimulate trade. In addition, what seems more relevant in a situation of un- and underemployment and a low marginal labour productivity in the backward countries is the income-generating effect of labour migration. Workers from backward areas earn their income in the coastal areas, remit their incomes to their home countries under conditions of full capital mobility and thus contribute to sustained import demand. The latter effect is expected to prevail in the WAEC.

Fourthly, compensation elements outside the framework of the WAEC were available through the so-called "Council of the Entente" financing development projects preferably in the backward states and funded - apart from external funds - more by Ivory Coast and Senegal than by the recipient countries.

In spite of such favourable preconditions an efficient intraregional division of labour did not materialise in the WAEC for several reasons. One package of problems comprises external shocks, overall economic policy failures in leading countries (e.g. public overspending in the Ivory Coast following the commodity price boom in the late 1970s), and corruption in the WAEC Secretariat. Apart from that, an essential mistake was the mélange of allocation and distribution policies in the main instrument of the WAEC, the so-called Taxe de Coopération Régionale (TCR). Like its model, the single tax (taxe unique) in the CACEU, the TCR is a substitute for customs duties on industrial imports from third countries and is levied on imports from member countries. It accrues to the consuming country, differs by enterprise, product and country and aims at establishing an automatic link with fiscal compensation for revenue losses due to trade diversion. Differences between hypothetical customs revenues gained from third country imports and TCR revenues are compensated through interbudgetary transfers effected through a Community Development Fund. Compensation is provided to the extent of two-thirds of assessed losses due to trade diversion. Fund revenues are paid by the member states according to their share in intraregional trade in TCR eligible products. The remaining one third is covered by discretionary contributions of the more advanced member states.

This complex system clearly aimed at limiting intraregional competition through tax differentiation between lower rates for backward countries' products and higher rates for advanced countries' products. It raised effective rates of protection through tax escalation and promoted regional import substitution through explicit discrimination against third country sources. Costs have been borne both by the backward countries keeping inefficient industries alive and by the more advanced member states protecting them against outside competition to the detriment of their international competitiveness.

It adds to the difficulties encountered by the WAEC that no external tariff could be established beyond an insignificant common duty in a two-tier tariff in which the much more important fiscal duties differ among the member states. Unilateral measures applied by backward members against imports from Senegal and Ivory Coast in recent years led to a further deviation from the customs union target (Synoptical Table A2). The willingness to compensate backward members for customs revenues foregone has declined since the Ivory Coast experienced an economic crisis.

What keeps the WAEC alive is the existence of the monetary union, the perception of having vested interests in forming a coalition against the political and economic potential of Nigeria within ECOWAS, and – most importantly – the access to external funds designed for cooperation projects such as a solar energy project.

3. The Economic Community of West African States

The Economic Community of West African States (ECOWAS/CEDEAO) founded in 1975 by all sixteen francophone, anglophone and lusophone West African states covering an area from Mauritania to Nigeria has received the largest attention of scholars interested in Sub-Saharan African integration. [1] Such attention can be explained by the sheer size of the Community (about 180 mill. inhabitants), by the ambitious character of bridging cultural, ethnical and language diversities and by the seeming attractiveness of studying pan-African integration en miniature.

However, this interest devoted to ECOWAS clearly contrasts with the achievements of this grouping. Though more than 90 per cent of total trade of ECOWAS members with African countries is within ECOWAS [World Bank, 1988], intraregional trade accounted but for 3.2 per cent of world exports of ECOWAS in 1986 (Table A3). Most intraregional trade is in primary commodities and would have also occurred without integration. Yet, recorded trade is only part of total trade since deficient trade statistics, smuggling and traditional border trade are wide-spread phenomena in ECOWAS [Igué, 1976, 1983; Akano, 1984; Deardorff, Stolper, 1990]. They reflect the magnitudes of differences in national sectoral policy interference and the low degree of macroeconomic policy coordination.

A number of ECOWAS members are marginal and counterproductive ones in the sense that they do not participate actively in the integration process but prevent the Community from implementing adopted decisions unanimously. By behaving in this way, they add a cost element to decision making. The discrepancy between Nigeria and the remaining fifteen members in terms of market size, production and trade is without any parallel in other integration groupings throughout the world. Nigeria offers an enormous potential of new export markets for the smaller countries provided they meet origin rules and competitive requirements. However, reluctance to open own markets to Nigerian products dominates over own export interests.

---

[1] E.g. Akinyemi et al. [1984]; Asante [1985; 1986]; Orimalade, Ubogu [1984]; Robson [1983].

Given such constraints multiplied by severe bottlenecks to trade in the infrastructure, ECOWAS has appeared as a poor candidate for trade integration from its very beginning but as a promising one for cooperation bringing some neighbouring countries together under an ECOWAS-wide institutional framework [Zehender, 1987, Chapter 3].

This judgment has proven to be correct. None of the liberalisation schedules were kept which were laid out in the Treaty as three stages towards the formation of a customs union to be terminated within fifteen years. Apart from political problems manifested in border conflicts or problems of economic decay following the decline in commodity prices, the difficulties of compromising on common trade preferences were underrated. Nomenclatures, tax levels and structures, valuation bases, origin rules and other important ingredients of border control differed widely and so did perceptions of minimum local equity shares in enterprises producing goods under Community treatment. Again, different perceptions emerged between francophone countries with relatively low local ownership in multinational corporations on the one hand and anglophone countries on the other hand where local ownership shares were more sizeable [Robson, 1983, p. 117-18].

Overall, ECOWAS was best characterised by the former Nigerian president Shagari who, in 1980, stated that protocols and decisions were not being ratified as fast as could reasonably be expected. Even those ratified were hardly implemented to spirit and letter [Africa Research Bulletin, 1980, No. 5, p. 6440].

This assessment has not lost its validity in a worsening economic environment in the 1980s. Some institutional achievements, such as the foundation of a West African Clearing House (operating on a very modest scale with declining transactions in recent years; Table A2) or cooperation in shipping, have failed to offset the setbacks [Robson, 1985, p. 619]. Among them, the most critical one was the expulsion of ECOWAS residents from Nigeria in 1985 which violated the immigration protocol adopted by ECOWAS members. Given such setbacks, ECOWAS activities recently turned towards new areas of economic cooperation, e.g. to the externally cosponsored regional telecommunication network, a customs computerisation programme pursued with assistance of the United Nations Conference on Trade and Development (UNCTAD), the United Nations

Development Programme (UNDP) and bilateral donors, and an ECOWAS cultural framework.

Furthermore, ECOWAS agreed to increase the callable capital of the ECOWAS Fund from US $ 90 mill. to US $ 360 mill. in order to enlarge its guarantee capacity and thereby to improve its fund-raising position. A so-called ECO-Bank, a cooperative project for the private sector enterprises started its operations primarily focusing on offshore banking [UNCTAD, b].

In spite of discouraging experiences with regional industrial programming, ECOWAS adopted an Industrial Development Programme in 1986 for the period 1987-1991 setting out essentially a programme of action to prepare a Multisectoral Master Plan.

To summarise, contrasting to its ambitious Treaty, ECOWAS has remained a dormant integration scheme which only recently seems to have taken into account the very high barriers to efficient regional integration. As trade effects are assessed to be low if not marginal, one cannot deny that ECOWAS instruments have not yet had discriminatory consequences for extra- and intraregional trade flows worth to be mentioned.

4. The Central African Customs and Economic Union

Until the mid-1970s the Central African Customs and Economic Union (CACEU/UDEAC) founded in 1964 and comprising Cameroon, Gabon, the Central African Republic (CAR), Congo, Chad, and later on Equatorial Guinea, was evaluated as a promising integration bloc which closely approached the stage of a customs union. The reasons for this assessment resemble those given for the WAEC: there were the colonially based patterns of close monetary cooperation (though the Central Bank of Central African States and the agreements with France did not arrive at a monetary union in a strict sense), a common external tariff negotiated in the 1960s between the member countries of the old ECU and the new member Cameroon, and - most importantly - the so-called single tax system as a substitute to internal customs duties similar to the TCR in the WAEC. Furthermore, the member countries negotiated a common investment code for industries of regional importance, participated in a common oil refinery for some time, and maintained a common river shipping agency also for some time.[1]

Yet, expectations did not materialise. Firstly, the single tax differing by origin and consumer countries for the same products as well as by enterprises had the same effect as the TCR. It promoted regional import substitution and sheltered marginal suppliers against competition from member countries. In addition, it raised the effective rate of protection of finished goods as inputs were imported duty-free, and imposed high costs of administration and enforcement of rules as tax evasion was to be avoided [Ekwe, 1987]. Ravenhill´s judgement [1985, p. 208] that the single tax system acted perversely to protect inefficient domestic industries and to encourage intraregional import substitution, is well-taken. Secondly, common projects such as the oil refinery and the shipping agency were given up. Thirdly, the former two-tier common external tariff with customs duties and fiscal duties became diluted by so-called supplementary taxes which differed by CACEU countries. Fourthly, no agreement could be reached with respect to labour mobility within the Union. Fifthly, common industrialisation planning on a regional scale failed for which the common investment code should pave the way. Sixthly, compensation instruments such as the Solidarity Fund implemented in the 1960s and early 1970s were abolished. Seventhly, investment in infrastructure such as the two new railway trunks (Transcamerounais and Transgabonais) remained national projects and failed to overcome the high natural protection rates which emerged because of inadequate conditions for surface transport. Eighthly, monetary cooperation and coordination could not be sustained on the high level achieved in francophone West Africa.

Parallel to these setbacks, the share of intraregional trade in total trade fell from 4 per cent in the first part of the 1970s to 2.8 per cent in 1986 (Table A3). New initiatives towards integration could not be launched in the past. This is indicated by the meagre results of summit meetings between 1985 and 1988 (Table A2). A basic revision of all integration instruments is under way and cooperation projects in software development (technology, agriculture, livestock, transport) have gained more attractiveness than in the past. Obviously, the CACEU is in a

---

[1] Langdon, Mytelka [1979]; Langhammer [1978]; Mytelka [1973]; Ndongko [1985]; Robson [1968]; Yondo [1970].

stalemate position as larger groupings in Central Africa which include Zaire seem to have more appeal (without coming to more concrete results, however). Expanding the country coverage of Central African groupings will have the effect of further lessening the trend towards a customs union while bilateral cooperation, e.g. between Zaire and Congo or between Cameroon, Gabon and the CAR, will be promoted.

From its very beginning the three crucial constraints of the CACEU were the outward orientation of the two primary commodity exporting countries Gabon and Congo, the - even by African standards - extra-ordinary economic weakness of the two backward members CAR and Chad, and high natural protection through an inadequate transportation network. Affiliates of multinational enterprises produce homogeneous goods in several member countries (e.g. footwear and clothing), and they are sheltered against competition among each other through both natural and policy-induced barriers. In those manufactured products where intraregional trade exists, market size in the backward countries is so small that "training ground" arguments, economies of scale or other dynamic effects have no meaning at all. In each CACEU member country it is solely the domestic market which matters for local producers.

5. The East African Community

The experiences of the East African Community (EAC) comprising Kenya, Tanzania and Uganda provide the deepest insights into the rise and decay of a grouping covering the whole spectrum of far-reaching trade integration cum compensation and common infrastructure policies. During the colonial period mainland Tanzania (the former Tanganyika) had achieved a common internal market together with the two other coun-tries. The Community included a common customs tariff, tax harmoni-sation, a monetary union, and common services (railway, ports, com-munication, universities, and other research institutes). Under such conditions but not necessarily because of them, Kenya developed to an industrial centre in the region.[1] Over time the Kenyan manufacturing

---

[1] Kenya enjoyed a better colonial status than the other member coun-tries. As a crown colony more resources were flowing into the coun-

sector found important market outlets in the two neighbouring countries thus supporting an intersectoral division of labour between the major exporter of manufactures and the two other member states exporting commodities and food products. The transition from colonial rule to independence paved the way towards disintegration in the 1960s when not only politicians but also scholars highlighted the question of net gainers from integration under zero-sum game assumptions.[1] Empirical analyses saying that Tanzania was a net loser due to integration were heavily disputed in academic circles but provided legitimacy for the two net importers Tanzania and Uganda to urge for compensation and finally to initiate the dissolution of the Community.

In the mid-1960s - still under the old rules of the pre-independence customs union - Kenya agreed to a number of measures restricting its intraregional exports and promoting its imports but this only led to stronger competition on the Kenyan domestic market and did not sizeably promote imports from Tanzania and Uganda. Financial compensation given in the so-called "Distributable Pool" also failed to contain the decay. So did a sharp intervention into intraregional trade through the introduction of border taxes (so-called transfer taxes) in 1967, when the Community was officially inaugurated. External shocks such as the oil price hike severely reduced the willingness of partners to secure financing of common services and coincided with growing internal disputes on economic order principles between socialist Tanzania and capitalist Kenya. Finally, the Amin rule and the "looking South to Zambia perception" of Tanzania contributed to the collapse of the Community which took a number of years until it was disbanded 1977, ten years after its foundation.

Lessons taught by the experiences of the EAC are fivefold. Firstly, disputes on the basics of macroeconomic management are deadly for a Community. When Tanzania firmly took its stance towards state planning against the relatively market-oriented system of Kenya, no compensation scheme was able to bridge the dissent.

---

tries, and an administrative network was established by the metropolitan power. It is subject to debate to what extent the superior development of Kenya was based on this advantage.

[1] Cf. Hazlewood [1975; 1979] summarising the work mainly done under his initiative at the Oxford Institute of Economics and Statistics.

Secondly, free circulation of labour can be an essential amalgam of regional integration. It was one of the very few prerequisites missing in the pre-Community stage of integration under colonial rule.

Thirdly, the dissolution of a monetary union as it happened in East Africa after 1961 provided scope for autonomous exchange-rate changes but failed to be effective when massive interventions into intraregional trade occured simultaneously.

Fourthly, the "training ground" argument of regional integration must be questioned again. Kenya never achieved international competitiveness of manufactured goods exported intraregionally.

Fifthly, common services in "hardware" (physical infrastructure) are vulnerable if the institutional management lies in the hands of the participating partners which take dissenting views about burden sharing. Probably, the distribution of benefits was conditioned by the level of economic development: Kenya as the more advanced partner could draw more benefits from common services than Tanzania and Uganda [Hazlewood, 1979]. Decentralisation of headquarters failed to offset this fundamental relation between economic development and transactions in services. Perhaps, the internationalisation of common services beyond the participating states could have saved them from decay.

6. The Southern African Development Coordination Conference

The Southern African Development Coordination Conference (SADCC) founded in 1980 by the five so-called frontline states Angola, Botswana, Mocambique, Zambia, and Tanzania and later on joined by Malawi, Lesotho, Swaziland, and Zimbabwe pursues a basically political objective, to coordinate measures aimed at reducing economic dependency on South Africa. This approach is mainly geared at capital-intensive regional cooperation in "hardware" (e.g. establishing an own transport network to become independent from South African railways). Given this objective, SADCC has to rely on external funds available to support a genuine political rather than an economic target. All this and the explicit renunciation of trade integration has made SADCC unique among African regional groupings. In fact, trade integration in this region is covered by the "sister" organisation PTA which widely overlaps with SADCC in membership. [1]

The record of summit meetings of SADCC during the period 1985–1988 (Synoptical Table A2) suggests that the political objective has not yet been fully shared by all members to the same extent. Countries maintaining strong economic relations with South Africa in trade, capital transactions and labour migration like Malawi and Lesotho abstained from summit meetings. Furthermore, even without these two members, sanctions against South Africa as the main political point on the summit agenda could not be agreed upon unanimously.

Economically, the SADCC has been successful in 1988 to commit external donors to financing regional projects in the transport and communication sector. This may cement regional cooperation between SADCC members at least until 1991. However, such external pump-priming cannot obscure the fact that internal cooperation is still very fragile. Recent experiences with the SADCC Food Security Program as one of the most important projects aiming at market stabilisation, regional trade and food aid do not seem to be encouraging. Hay and Rukuni [1988] conclude that it has been easier to define the benefits of regional collaboration than to capture them. Its success is said to rest to a more critical extent on the level of confidence existing among member states than on the technical and financial capacity to pursue its objectives. The coherence of the SADCC grouping is assumed to be still too fragile to permit rapid progress as policies are strongly identified with ideologies which are very different among the members. Slow progress in the programme is linked to the emerging danger that the programme is seen by member states as an additional means by which they can gain access to investment funds for their own national development. As a result of this priority for national development, there are incentives to identify regional benefits for what are essentially national plans so that they qualify for regional support [ibid., p. 1021].

Additionally, the existence of a well-performing member country in the agricultural sector with good natural, physical and human resource endowment, which is Zimbabwe among its malaise-ridden neighbours, has

---

[1] For details on the early history of SADCC, cf. Zehender [1983].

made cooperation more sensitive and touchy. And finally, reliance on regional rather than national supply does not yet seem to be undisputed as the proposal of Zimbabwe has witnessed to extend energy supply from its Kariba South hydroelectric station despite the availability of surplus electricity on the Zambian side of the scheme. [1]

To summarise, SADCC in its present form seems still far from being a grouping with clearly defined objectives, efficient instruments on a regional scale and a good implementation record. While external shocks and internal noneconomic problems like famines, droughts, disruptive civil conflicts and the confrontation with South Africa cannot be denied to have contributed to the disappointing results, the deep-rooted ideological differences between the members should not be underrated. They require a broadening (and growing vagueness) of objectives defined and compromising on instruments applied as the Food Security Program has demonstrated. More conflicts as those having emerged until now could be contained by easy access to external public funds which enable "shopping lists" to be implemented. Should access to external funds become inelastic, however, SADCC will be exposed to stronger internal pressures. Then, it will have to pass the test whether regional cooperation can be initiated with own funds and beyond purely political targets.

7. The Preferential Trade Area of Eastern and Southern African States

The Preferential Trade Area of Eastern and Southern African States (PTA) which was constituted in 1981 can be understood as the regional trade department of SADCC whose member states form the nucleus of PTA. Additionally, seven countries (Burundi, Comoros, Ethiopia, Kenya, Mauritius, Rwanda, and Somalia) acceded the PTA while Angola was the only SADCC member which abstained from PTA membership until late 1989.

Though the PTA comprises members of failed or still existing institutions such as the EAC or the Community of the Great Lakes or the old South African Customs Union (SACU), this grouping does not and cannot

---

[1] Cf. consultative meeting of January 1988 in Arusha (Synoptical Table A2).

claim to act as a successor of any of these institutions. Given the extra-ordinary heterogeneity of the grouping ranging from remote island states like Comoros to core countries like Zambia, Kenya and Zimbabwe, the multilateral approach to trade integration was not feasible from the very beginning. Instead, trade concessions with most-favoured nation treat-ment within the region were introduced, which were designed in a way that only very few countries were able to benefit from these concessions. As a result, no more than 50 per cent of Heads of States participated in each of the annual summit meetings between 1985 and 1988 (Synoptical Table A2). Under such circumstances the adoption of programmes has no meaning as missing member states do not adhere to them.

In every aspect, the record of the PTA reflects a typical sequence of all African groupings regardless whether they aim at cooperation or integration: a dynamic initial phase of launching various programmes and institutions (such as a common list for products to be liberalised, a PTA Clearing House and a PTA Development Bank) is followed by a phase of implementation and ratification problems or even nonimplementation.

In the PTA, the implementation of the trade-liberalisation programme was seriously delayed by dissenting views on the provisions limiting preferences to companies with majority equity holdings of nationals of member states. The 1986 summit approved a sophisticated three-tier system with preference margins increasing with local ownership which widened the scope for red tape.

Another shortcoming of the PTA has been the failure to dismantle administrative barriers in the clearance of transit transport. Govern-mental decisions to accept a single Road Customs Transit Document in the PTA and to introduce a so-called PTA Third Party Motor Vehicle Liability Insurance Scheme for facilitating transit trade are simply not passed down the ranks so that arbitrary decisions ultimately rest with the customs posts.

Administration of import licencing arrangements is reported to be an additional source of disputes in the PTA. Bilateral open general import licence arrangements between PTA member countries had to be cancelled because the PTA membership does not allow closed-ended bilateral ar-rangements. This led to a decline of trade between members like Malawi and Zimbabwe [World Bank, 1988c, p. 52]. Furthermore, "tied" credit lines granted by foreign donors do not allow for a preferential use of import licencing to the advantage of PTA members. Foreign exchange shortages have been assessed as a major reason of restrictive import licencing. Clearing arrangements through the Harare-based PTA Clearing House were intended to ease this problem for intra-PTA trade as the provisions for these arrangements do not require full cash settlement. However, the 1987 Summit stated as a main problem that the facilities were still insufficiently used. Notwithstanding arrears in balance settlement, the major problem still remains that import licences are discretionarily allocated in favour of so-called essential goods imported from outside the PTA. PTA-originating goods, on the other hand, are frequently regarded as nonessential goods that could be replaced by domestic production. Irrespective of the allocation of import licences there is a clear trade diversion bias in the selection of products eligible for trade preferences as at least one member state must document its official "import interest". It is very likely that such an interest will be denied if local producers are exposed to competition from intraregional suppliers and be announced only if extraregional imports can be replaced.

Shortcomings have not deterred the governments of PTA member states to go ahead. Two major plans were launched recently. Firstly, a schedule for intra-PTA liberalisation was approved at the 1987 Summit to the effect that between 1988 and 1996 tariffs should be reduced by 10 per cent annually. Secondly, traveller cheques denominated in PTA Currency Units (PTACU) were introduced in 1988 compulsory for all travellers within the region in order to facilitate commercial exchanges and to set local businessmen free from current exchange restrictions. Both clearing arrangements and the removal of payments restrictions are based on external policy advice granted to PTA members [Anjaria et al., 1982]. Again, the basic problem rests with implementation apart from well-founded doubts whether such institutional arrangements really cure the crucial barriers to trade within the PTA, that is a vast amount of NTBs often arbitrarily applied.

Prospects for the PTA mainly arise from existing trade relations between neighbouring countries such as Malawi, Zimbabwe, Botswana, and Zambia. Major trade creating effects, however, are very unlikely to occur if the distinction between "essential" goods from non-PTA sources and "nonessential" goods from PTA sources remains effective. Given the current economic crisis in almost all member states, the existence of the

PTA is critically linked to access to foreign funds and expertise on all aspects of customs clearance, invoicing and transit trade.

IV. Regional Integration in the Middle East and Asia

1. The Basics of Regional Integration in the Middle East and Asia

Regional integration as well as cooperation schemes in the Middle East and Asia have never gained such attractiveness compared to Latin America and Sub-Saharan Africa. Political as well as economic factors bear responsibility for this fact. Politically, countries in the two regions often confronted themselves in a state of hostility where the political rationale of defining common targets became overshadowed by blunt nationalism. In those instances where common external challenges gave scope for some initiatives as in North Africa and the Middle East, they soon proved to be either pure rhetorics or ill-conceived blueprints without any substance.

Economically, the enormous heterogeneity of countries raised concern of unequal distribution of benefits. The region hosts huge entities at different levels of industrialisation and income like Indonesia, India and China, prosperous outward-oriented city states like Hong Kong and Singapore, resource-rich economies exporting the same products like the oil-exporting countries, dynamic resource-poor achievers like Taiwan and South Korea, least developed countries like Nepal and Bangladesh as well as middle-income countries which try to manage the take-off from commodity exporters to efficient producers of manufactures.

Except for the traditional division of labour between primary commodity exporters and exporters of manufactures which does not require integration schemes, the degree of complementarity among Asian and Middle Eastern countries has been low. The same applies to infrastructure networks. All countries were individual achievers in exchange with industrialised economies rather than team achievers. In most cases, this option did not prove to be unsuccessful so that the integration argument was beaten by the evidence of individual performance. Ambitious plans like the design of an Arab Common Market or a Maghreb Customs Union thus remained paper work. Even modest integration approaches like preferential tariff reductions on an item-by-item basis like the Bangkok Agreement between Bangladesh, India, Lao People's Democratic Republic, South Korea, and Sri Lanka failed to produce results worth mentioning.

Instead of integration, cooperation has recently found more interest in the two regions as it is witnessed by the emergence of the Gulf Co-operation Council (GCC) with Bahrain, Kuwait, Oman, Qatar, Saudi Arabia, and the United Arab Emirates as well as of the South Asian Association for Regional Co-operation (SAARC) set up between Bangla-desh, Bhutan, India, the Maldives, Nepal, Pakistan, and Sri Lanka in 1981. Both schemes still provide little more than an institutional umbrella and thus will not be analysed in the following. Yet, they underline that interests are strongly in favour of economic cooperation and not of inte-gration. Therefore, in the following only two schemes are shortly intro-duced which pursued very different approaches of either private goods-based intraregional cooperation (Regional Co-operation for Development) or public goods-based extraregional cooperation (ASEAN).

2. The Regional Co-operation for Development

From its beginning in 1964, the Regional Co-operation for Develop-ment (RCD) between Iran, Turkey and Pakistan renounced to formulate ambitious liberalisation schedules. Instead, RCD confined itself to pro-mote trade among the partner countries pragmatically, i.e. on a bilateral level and in sectors where common interests could be defined. In addi-tion, the grouping aimed at cooperating in transport and communication, and it is in these sectors where it could achieve notable results during the period 1964-1976.[1] The wide interest which the RCD gained during this period, however, can be derived from another instrument which scholars like Little [1966] and Brewster [1971] had recommended as a second-best model if full integration of a region in the shape of a com-mon market could not be achieved. So-called joint purpose enterprises (JPEs) in which private agents and/or statals or parastatals would

---

[1] Cf. the very detailed description of Bahadir [1984, pp. 300-339] and the periodical publication of annual RDC reports and newsletters cited in Bahadir.

finance part of the equity capital were thought to help creating an element of regional interest and solidarity [Little, 1966, p. 181]. The RCD implemented some JPEs which were characterised by relatively strong public interference, e. g. public ownership, long-term purchase or sourcing guarantees given by nonproducing member states, and guarantees referring to profit participation and repatriation in currencies in which the equity payment was made. Purchase or sourcing guarantees acted as substitutes for preferential tariff treatment and thus stimulated more trade diversion than would have been possible under conditions of preference margins only.

Until the early 1970s, the RCD implemented three enterprises with joint equity participation of at least two member states: an enterprise producing bank notes and security paper in Karachi, an aluminium company producing aluminium bars in Tehran on the basis of commodities imported from RCD member states, and a ball bearing industry in Karachi. During the 1970s, eight other JPEs began to operate, however, only under national ownership and with long-term purchase guarantees. By 1980, another nine industries were in the stage of planning.

After the Iranian revolution in 1979 the RCD came to a standstill; even a formal dissolution was discussed but not implemented. Initiatives to reactivate the RCD came from Iran in 1984. Under a new heading called Economic Co-operation Organization (ECO), new fields of common interest in hardware and software cooperation have been explored, but hitherto with little result given the extraordinary internal and external constraints the region has to cope with.

With these sudden breaks in the history of the RCD, an assessment of experiences is practically impossible. Intraregional trade volumes are no adequate yardsticks as trade integration was not aimed at. Intraregional trade shares never exceeded 1 or 2 per cent during the RCD period, and the sudden jump to 10 per cent after 1984 in the ECO period (Table A3) has nothing to do with integration but simply reflects the dramatic decline of the Iranian trade volume during the Gulf war and the continuation of bilateral commodity trade between Turkey and Iran.

More telling is the fact that plans to merge the three national airlines or to link the three capitals by means of a railway trunk never approached the stage of implementation. The JPEs were a very first approach of sectoral industrialisation planning on a regional level. This approach was bound to end in an impasse given the diverging interests of producing and non-producing countries and the shortcomings of planning on a national level in the three countries. What emerged as the outcome of planning "from the top" is that the JPE strategy failed to attract private capital owners, as it was the initial target of the RCD Chamber of Commerce and Industry founded as an intermediary between private sectors in the member states. Full reliance on public ownership, however, meant subordination of production of private goods under political objectives which changed rapidly when the leading force in the RCD, the Iran, entered a period of revolution followed by the Gulf war.

3. The Association of Southeast Asian Nations

The Association of Southeast Asian Nations (ASEAN) founded by Indonesia, Malaysia, the Philippines, Singapore and Thailand in 1967 and joined by Brunei in 1984 is by far the most successful Asian integration and cooperation scheme. This success can be measured in terms of worldwide reputation and acceptance of ASEAN by OECD members as a permanent dialogue partner.

At first glance it is amazing that ASEAN owes this standing neither to the formation of a uniform trading bloc with supranational sovereignty in trade policies nor to the advancement of regional industrialisation schemes with JEPs as in the RCD case. In both aspects, ASEAN has failed to meet expectations.[1]

With respect to trade, the member countries initially agreed on a Preferential Trading Arrangement (PTA) and recently - on the occasion of the third ASEAN Summit in December 1987 - scheduled an improvement of the PTA in terms of product coverage and depth of tariff cuts. However, tariff preferences do not play a significant role in intra-ASEAN trade, and it is very unlikely that this will change in the future. This assessment is first witnessed by the fact that no regular statistical record on the amount of intra-ASEAN trade receiving preferences exists. An approximate information referring to intraregional exports supported

---

[1] For comprehensive overviews on ASEAN achievements, cf. ASEAN [1987a; 1987b] and Sopiee et al. [1987].

by rules-of-origin certificates suggests that this trade had amounted to only US $ 45 mill. in 1982 [quoted in Chng, 1985, p. 33], that is 1 per cent of total intra-ASEAN non-oil exports. The overwhelming part of intra-ASEAN trade (Table A4) occurs either in primary commodities not eligible for preferential treatment, or in entrepôt trade, or in manufactures which do not meet rules of origin requirements [Rieger, 1985]. Rules of origins are important in a PTA where tariff protection levels differ widely among the partner countries, not only in the special case of Singapore as an almost free trade area but also between Indonesia and Malaysia. Such rules restrictively applied have enabled the ASEAN countries to improve the PTA "at the surface" without exposing domestic industries to intensified regional competition as most of the eligible products do not meet the rules. Thus, in spite of extended product coverage and larger preference margins the PTA will remain widely ineffective unless rules of origin are not substantially liberalised. However, even if this should occur it will remain doubtful whether TBs are really an important impediment to intra-ASEAN trade. Recent empirical evidence has supported the view that there is much water in legal tariff rates [Langhammer, 1988] and that NTBs are looked upon as the more relevant obstacles to trade by ASEAN traders [Sanchez, 1987].

As far as the second major field of action within ASEAN is concerned, i. e. economic cooperation, a distinction has to be made between internal industrial cooperation and external cooperation in areas of common interest. Internal industrial cooperation became mainly influenced by the recommendations of a UN mission in the early 1970s [UN, 1974] in favour of large-scale regional industrial projects. Subsequently, three basic instruments were developed, each one designed as a substitute of a former approach which failed. The first instrument was framed as so-called ASEAN Industrial Projects (AIPs), i. e. five large scale industrial plants to be located in each of the five founding member states (two urea projects in Indonesia and Malaysia, a diesel engine plant in Singapore, a super phosphate plant in the Philippines, and a soda-ash project in Thailand). None of these AIPs was implemented as no agreement could be reached on the monopoly rights claimed by such regional industries. As a substitute, the ASEAN Industrial Complementation Scheme (AIC) was launched by ASEAN governments in 1980 which was intended to be a package of various forward and backward linked products. At least four member countries were intended to participate in such a package, e.g. in the automotive industry. Again, AICs never arrived at the stage of implementation. The third and least ambitious scheme was the ASEAN Industrial Joint Venture (AIJV), in which residents from at least two member countries should hold a majority ownership of at least 51 per cent in order to qualify for preferential treatment and other privileges. The record of the AIJVs is less obvious than that of the AIPs and the AICs but it seems that in spite of improvements of privileges agreed upon by the ASEAN Summit in December 1987 the AIJVs have not been attractive to local businessmen. Some approvals of AIJVs were given but whether intended industrial cooperation between private capital owners from various ASEAN member states was really implemented has remained open. In total, the record of industrial cooperation within ASEAN has been discouraging.

To summarise, ASEAN owes its worldwide acceptance as a dialogue partner for OECD countries not to its progress in internal integration and industrial cooperation but to other factors. To mention four of them:

Firtstly, ASEAN was founded as an institution to formulate and represent commcn interests of its members in foreign affairs (Vietnam, Kampuchea). It succeeded to generate common positions on these issues and to sustain these positions over a longer period of time.

Secondly, its member countries shared common views on the principles of a division of labour between the private and the public sector. Basically, all ASEAN member countries were efficiency-oriented and - as a region - belonged to the most prosperous economic entities in the world throughout two decades. Again, this perception of market forces as the driving element of development is still accepted in the member countries and has become even stronger as a policy guideline over time [Hughes, 1989].

Thirdly, ASEAN member countries have established a strong internal network of consultations and software cooperation without surrendering national sovereignty in major economic policies. This network contributes to lower costs of information and makes national policies more predictable for neighbouring countries.

Fourthly, ASEAN runs permanent dialogues with the major OECD countries on market accessibility and achieved some success in raising its collective bargaining power, e.g. in dialogues with the EC on the Generalised System of Preferences (GSP) and the Multi Fibre Agreement (MFA) [Langhammer, 1985].

As a relatively small grouping in terms of members trends towards bilateralism have not been as strong in ASEAN as in other integration schemes. Probably, the fact that ASEAN was more outward-oriented in its objectives and from the very beginning far less ambitious with respect to internal integration than for instance the LAFTA has contributed to more multilateralism. Software cooperation, e.g. in science and technology, culture and information, social development, and sectoral policies, is institutionally channelled throughout respective ASEAN committees and has received increasing attention [ASEAN, 1988].

V. Recent Changes in RIDC

RIDC has experienced a number of new approaches and initiatives in the 1980s which have not yet been fully implemented in many cases. To evaluate them, three strands of changes - compared to the 1960s and 1970s - can be sketched:

1) There has been a shift from preannounced internal integration schedules via free trade areas, customs unions and common markets to less binding project-oriented cooperation schemes.

2) Within integration arrangements options for pursuing regional trade liberalisation "at different speeds" were widened allowing individual members to proceed more rapidly than others, to negotiate bilateral preferences with partners sharing common sectoral interests and to keep such agreements open to other member countries for future participation.

3) Within cooperation schemes regional industrialisation planning or programming lost its priority compared to cooperation in hardware (e.g. physical infrastructure, communication, transport) or in software (training, research, technology).

The shift to cooperation schemes is visible in all major regional groupings. There is no scheme today which has not learnt the lesson that copying the example of the EC does not work under conditions prevailing in developing countries. The straightforward way to liberalising goods and factor movements by pre-committing the members to a stages approach has been left. Instead of binding schedules, discretionary actions prevail.

Alternatives (2) and (3) have emerged in the various groupings. Schemes geared at dismantling internal barriers to imports from member countries at a multilateral level have provided more leeway for bilateralism.

The outstanding example in Latin America is the case of Brazil-Argentina in the framework of LAIA. Institutionalised cooperation started in 1983 and since that time has materialised in an agreement on duty-free bilateral trade. By the end of 1990, at least 50 per cent of capital goods traded between the two countries are to be granted preferential access. A 1988 arrangement specifies upper limits for bilateral trade imbalances in preferential trade. They are intended to free the agreement in its operation from the well-known distribution conflicts. Even more important than the tariff cuts is the intended dismantling of NTBs for up to 50 per cent of total trade in industrial food products until 1993.

Examples for alternative (3) are schemes like the Andean Group or ASEAN which have switched from regional industrialisation to other means of cooperation.

These developments have similar implications for the decision-making process. If ever supranational authorities had power to decide or to fix rules, this power has vanished. National authorities have regained or maintained their rights to decide. Common secretariats either have mailbox functions only or provide technical assistance to national governments.

The variety of common projects has largely increased in the course of cooperation with multi-tier axles and so has the demand for technical expertise and financial resources along with the process of replacing integration by cooperation. Demand can often not be satisfied from regional sources. This holds especially for Sub-Saharan African groupings where expertise and resources keeping the schemes alive have been increasingly imported from nonmember countries, e.g. OECD countries and the Arab oil exporters. Such reliance on external funds gives rise to concerns that the necessity of self-defining common projects and bearing the responsibility of funding them from own resources is watered as is the internal clearing process of burden sharing.

E. Lessons from the Experiences with RIDC

I. The Balance of Failure and Success

The analysis of RIDC presented in Chapter D leads to the conclusion that the expected benefits from regional integration (Chapter B) have not materialised. Irrespective of initial political and economic conditions and despite numerous integration and cooperation efforts, RIDC has failed to offer a viable development strategy for the catching-up process. If member countries of integration schemes have achieved sustained economic growth and social development such as the Southeast Asian countries, Brazil, and Kenya as well as the Ivory Coast in the 1960s and early 1970s, they were not successful because of RIDC but in spite of RIDC. RIDC has at best promoted trade diversion and a prolonged process of inefficient regional import substitution.

The reasons for the failure of RIDC are internal rather than external. International economic conditions deteriorated in the 1970s and 1980s, but the roots of disintegration can be traced back to the late 1960s and early 1970s, before the first oil price shock hit. Cases in point are the 1968 crisis of LAFTA, the break-down of the CACM in 1969, the suspension of duty-free intraregional trade in the EAC in 1967, or the distributional conflicts paralysing the CACEU in 1968. External factors may have prevented a revitalisation of stagnating integration efforts; however, they did not cause stagnation or even disintegration. RIDC failed because integration policies were implemented half-heartedly and often in an inconsistent fashion, were abolished after a relatively short period of time, or were neutralised by new, mostly NTBs:

- Member countries of most so-called customs unions did never grant duty-free market access to each other, and efforts towards trade liberalisation were either limited to more or less redundant TBs or were aborted early. Even customs unions inherited from the colonial past such as the EAC and the two francophone Unions in West and Central Africa soon broke up after the member states gained independence or disintegrated because new tariffs or NTBs were erected.
- Regional investment planning was high on the agenda of integration schemes in Latin America, Africa and Asia. A multitude of different

joint projects was envisaged and in many cases even agreed upon in ministerial meetings, but most of them were never carried out because of disputes over financing or management issues. Some projects that were actually carried out soon lost their economic importance since one or more of the initial partners decided to set up competing units in their own countries (e. g. production of tyres in the CACM or the common oil refinery in the CACEU).

- And finally, the internal mechanics of RIDC were not sufficiently developed. Compensation schemes for weak partner countries and clearing facilities were either not established or available funds had remained utterly insufficient to provide incentives for regional trade liberalisation. Likewise, adjustments of macroeconomic policies which would have been a prerequisite for regional trade creation did not make much progress. In particular, necessary exchange rate changes which could improve the competitive position of weak partner countries have remained halfhearted or were entirely avoided.

What remains on the asset side of RIDC are such intangibles as an improved flow of information across borders that may improve mutual understanding, and some scattered examples of relatively successful regional cooperation such as the joint bargaining of ASEAN countries in international trade negotiations, the joint efforts to attract foreign aid by SADCC and ECOWAS, as well as common projects to solve specific bilateral or multilateral problems (Interstate Committee to Fight Drought in the Sahel; ASEAN cooperation in training, research and communication). Measured in terms of the initial expectations associated with RIDC these "successes" have to be rated as by-products while the main product was not delivered.

II. Political Reasons for Failure

RIDC among independent nations entails a certain loss of sovereignty for each member country. This has proven to be a stumbling bloc for integration among young independent nations, particularly in Sub-Saharan Africa. The colonial heritage often combined with the necessity to forge a national consensus among rival tribes or social groups has made governments of these countries extremely reluctant to forego even minor

parts of their newly acquired political independence. Thus, the implementation of integration policies was sacrificed on the altar of a new
nationalism.

Such political constraints to regional integration were exacerbated in
cases of political instability and border conflicts. Civil war and social
unrest (El Salvador, Nicaragua) left attempts towards a CACM hanging
in the air, as did bilateral military conflicts such as between Honduras
and El Salvador in 1969. Latin American integration efforts suffered from
successive military coups in various countries (Argentina, Brazil, Chile,
Peru) while similar events (Burkina Faso, Ghana, Liberia, Mali, Nigeria)
have undermined African economic integration schemes [UN, 1988]. Re-
current border conflicts among East and West African countries constituted another impediment to integration in Sub-Saharan Africa.

In addition to nationalism and political instability, contradictory
political ideologies, i.e. a lacking consensus on a market-oriented approach, has been a reason for stagnating or abolished integration. Cases
in point were central planning in Tanzania or Peru versus market economy in Kenia and Chile. All in all, however, political obstacles to RIDC
should not be overestimated. Political problems have been decisive for
not implementing integration policies in some countries at certain times,
but they do not provide a sufficient explanation why RIDC has not
yielded the desired results across continents and over time.

III. Economic Reasons for Failure

1. A Deteriorating External Economic Environment

The establishment of customs unions or common markets among
developing countries requires an adjustment of production structures and
at least some degree of policy reform in each member country. Focal
points are incentives for new private investment as well as budgetary
and monetary discipline. The willingness of governments to shoulder the
burden of restructuring the private and the public sector depends,
among other things to be discussed below, on budgetary and balance-of-
payments constraints under which these governments have to operate.
Experience in both industrialised and developing countries shows that

adjustment is much easier to accomplish under conditions of buoyant external demand and steadily expanding export revenues. For RIDC, a prosperous and stable external environment is particularly important since intraregional trade and capital flows are not able to offset a recessional impact of world markets in the short to medium run given the initially low shares of intraregional economic transactions.

Viewed from this perspective, world economic conditions have not been very favourable to RIDC in the last two decades. Successive deep economic recessions in industrialised countries (1967/68, 1975/76, 1981/82), the two oil price shocks and a considerable slow down of world trade growth in the 1970s and 1980s compared to the 1960s have added to the volatility of export earnings and aggravated balance of payments problems for many developing countries [cf. e.g. Nunnenkamp, 1986, Chapter 5]. Exporters of manufactures in Latin America and Asia had to surmount increasing protectionist barriers in OECD countries while their import bill soared due to higher oil prices. Commodity dependent countries in Central America and in Africa suffered from volatile commodity prices and a secular decline of their barter terms of trade.

Price instability has caused concern because it is believed to raise risks for traders, producers and consumers and to contribute to the instability of export earnings, imports, investment and government expenditure. For example, through licence fees, export taxes, government-owned companies and marketing boards, primary commodity production is a major source of government revenues. These revenues become, therefore, almost as volatile as the commodity prices, hampering budget planning, and increasing the risk of large deficits and stop-and-go spending policies with detrimental effects on long-term public investment programmes and the riskiness of private investment. In such a framework, the implementation of integration policies may indeed become ineffectual.

According to the World Bank [1986], the terms of trade movements of commodity dependent countries have in general followed closely the real price trends. The barter terms of trade for major developing country regions show a general decline over the past decades. The decline has been especially severe for Africa, which has a large number of commodity exporting developing countries. On the other hand, the movement of the income terms of trade show substantial differences between regions. This suggests that Southeast Asia, for example, has been able

to increase productivity and volume of exports to maintain or even increase revenues from commodity exports despite unfavourable price
movements. In Africa, income terms of trade have remained in line with
barter terms of trade suggesting that the adverse export price developments have rather been aggravated by low or declining growth in export
volumes. This can reflect low productivity in the production of commodities and/or a loss of market shares to more competitive or aggressive
exporters of the same commodities in other regions.

Another important impediment to RIDC is rooted in the increasing
(private and public) debt burden of many Latin American and African
countries. High debt service obligations have made external financing
more difficult and have cut investment programmes via related austerity
measures. Much of the foreign debt had been incurred when export
prices were higher and the medium-term outlook for exports more buoy-
ant. As the terms of trade deteriorated, the burden of debt service
grew. In part, these developments were connected, as countries resorted
to increased borrowing in order to finance urgent imports and to meet
maturing debt obligations. The consequences of this borrowing was that
the debt of these countries rose rapidly relative to their export earnings, as did interest payments. The (net) effect of these developments
has been to impose severe adjustment and import restraints. As a result,
incomes have been reduced and development programmes disrupted.
Furthermore, countries facing a debt crisis reduced their willingness to
hold nonconvertible assets and urged for shorter settlement periods in
multilateral clearing arrangements. This behaviour contributed to the
suspension of the arrangements.

Whether or not the undeniably detrimental external developments
have had a decisive influence on the ability of developing countries to
implement integration policies remains doubtful, though. This doubt is
based on the observation that individual countries have performed very
differently under the same external threats. Empirical studies on the
presumed negative impact of price and earnings volatility on growth have
been inconclusive [MacBean, Nguyen, 1987]. Instability in export earnings may be only one, and not necessarily a dominant influence on economic growth, and the impact on investment, imports and income was
very different among countries, reflecting also offsetting policy actions
supported by adequate reserves or external borrowing. It is also note-

worthy that commodity dependent countries which have experienced higher growth rates of real gross domestic product (GDP) in 1980-1986 than in the previous period (1965-1980) have been faced with falling barter terms of trade while all those countries which were expected to benefit from rising terms of trade performed worse [OECD, 1989, p. 14]. And finally, manufactured exports from Southeast Asia and countries like Brazil have continued to expand at a rapid pace despite slower world trade growth and increasing protectionism in industrialised countries. The conclusion is that the deteriorating external environment was harmful to economic development and made adjustment more difficult, but the evidence seems to point to the importance of other factors than the external environment in explaining stagnating or disrupted integration efforts.

a. Barriers to Trade and Factor Mobility

It has been frequently mentioned above (Chapters D and E. I) that more intraregional specialisation did not materialise because there was a strong resistance in virtually all regional groupings against a significant reduction of TBs and impediments to factor mobility. In Sub-Saharan Africa, ECOWAS has consistently failed to implement decisions concerning trade liberalisation. In recent tariff reforms in Nigeria and Ghana, no account was taken of the agreement to initially freeze and then lower tariffs to ECOWAS members. Similar experiences have been made in the CACEU where the taxe unique became an effective import duty, and in the PTA where there was hardly any preferential trade in the subregion after the PTA was established [Granberg, 1985]. Unwillingness to implement trade liberalisation is by no means restricted to Africa, though. CARICOM has failed to agree on the implementation of the previously agreed elimination of all TBs within the region, and ASEAN has not been very successful in the mutual dismantling of TBs either.

This resistance against external liberalisation is all the more important since barriers to trade and factor mobility are usually much higher among developing countries than in industrialised countries. This applies in particular to TBs and NTBs [World Bank, 1987, Chapter 8]. In some regions, NTBs also tend to be much more variable in scope and extent so that effective protection fluctuates significantly from year to year as the result of the allocation of import licences and foreign exchange authorisations. High barriers to trade discourage export expansion in general, and differences among barriers to trade of developing and industrialised countries provide an incentive for extraregional instead of intraregional trade.

In a similar vain, most regional groupings have maintained extensive restrictions against capital flows and the movement of labour. Under current circumstances trade is unlikely to promote investment for production in the importing country. It is also difficult to rationalise production through takeovers, mergers and acquisitions and this sustains high costs that require extensive protection from imports. Foreign firms also often face regulatory and tax frameworks different from those confronted by domestic firms. Especially in low-income countries, large segments of the manufacturing sector tend to be reserved for public enterprises. Likewise, immigration rules or job entry regulations prevent labour to move from backward to more prosperous countries within the regional grouping as it would happen within a country to the benefit of both backward and prosperous areas. Thus, labour mobility has been confined to informal markets and specific sectors such as seasonal agricultural labour migration between Burkina Faso and the Ivory Coast.

Factor mobility is not a substitute but rather an engine of trade expansion [Hiemenz, Langhammer et al., 1987, Chapter D]. Investment in the partner country often complements domestic production and improves the intraregional specialisation. Labour movements can help to alleviate labour shortages in prospering countries, and income remittances increase demand in the home countries of migrant labour. All these opportunities have not been exploited in RIDC. Recently, only the ASEAN countries have undertaken some very cautious steps towards facilitating the transfer of capital among member countries [ASEAN, 1988, pp. 17-20].

b. *Macroeconomic Policies*

The most serious impediments to greater regional economic cooperation and trade have emerged from unintended side-effects of inappropriate and uncoordinated macroeconomic policies. An excessive reliance on public sector activities at the expense of the private sector has resulted in expansionary fiscal and monetary policies which in turn have strengthened inflationary pressures and an accumulation of public debt. The undesirable consequences were overvalued exchange rates and a crowding out of private investors. Overvalued exchange rates have the twofold disadvantage of discriminating against exports and of reducing and destabilising imports. This holds as export prices in foreign currency are artificially increased, and the shortage of foreign exchange associated with overvaluation requires rationing of foreign exchange available for imports. Both the wrong price signals and rationing tend to discourage intraregional trade. Imports from partner countries may be too expensive compared to other suppliers, and rationing usually favours suppliers of essential raw materials (oil) and investment goods in industrialised countries or the Middle East.

Another impediment to the expansion of intraregional trade arises from the lacking convertibility of national currencies which is a corollary to inappropriate macroeconomic policies. Nonconvertibility increases transaction costs of traders and investors, in particular when there are foreign exchange shortages. To remedy this problem, several regional groupings have maintained monetary unions or introduced clearing arrangements as second-best solutions [for details, cf. Fischer, 1983; Appendix Table 3]. The West African monetary union under the auspices of the French Central Bank is the main survivor of attempts to facilitate financing by maintaining fixed exchange rates among member countries. However, there is ample evidence for various member countries of the Franc Zone that fixed exchange rates have resulted in an overvaluation of the common currency, albeit to a different degree in different countries [Devarajan, Melo, 1987; Milner, 1990], and that access to French capital markets can - at least no longer - offset the damaging effects of overvaluation. Overvaluation is also the major reason why the CACEU, despite using a convertible currency, has much less intraregional trade than other groupings with more binding foreign exchange constraints.

Clearing arrangements have not proven to provide a solution to foreign exchange shortages either. A major reason was that financial balances tilted in favour of the dominating partner countries which were not prepared to keep large amounts of nonconvertible currencies in their portfolio. Further problems arose since financial resources for credit arrangements remained limited as refinancing in international capital markets suffered from the low creditworthiness of member countries.

c. *Low Gains from Integration*

Efforts towards RIDC, no matter whether they were undertaken in Asia, Africa or Latin America, have always been crippled by the fear of economic domination by a large or more advanced partner country. Typical examples were Nigeria within ECOWAS or Brazil within LAFTA. ASEAN economic integration stagnated because it was sandwiched between highly industrialised Singapore and poor, but vast Indonesia. The fear of domination grew out of the belief that integration should lead to "balanced" growth with an "equal" share of industry in each member country. This is, however, a mistaken proposition if economic integration is to improve resource use and allocation and hence, leads to a concentration of certain industries in one or another member country. Therefore, the income distribution among member countries may not necessarily improve in short to medium run since weaker members may loose inefficient industries established behind protective barriers and incur losses of government revenues from tariffs and taxes as a result of trade liberalisation.

In such a situation, weaker member countries stand to loose from integration initially and will demand financial compensation from more successful members. Such compensation schemes have actually been established in the WAEC, the CACEU and the EAC, but they could not prevent a final stalemate of integration efforts in these groupings. The reason for this failure was that compensation payments were considered to be inadequate by weaker members and/or that stronger members were not prepared to shoulder a higher burden. The economic rationale of this result is easily explained. Weaker members suffer from trade liberalisation in the first round while benefits from improved specialisation take time to materialise, in particular when factors of production are not allowed to move freely as was the case in most regional groupings. More advanced countries have already entered, at least to some degree, in the international division of labour and benefit only marginally from trade and other concessions granted by the weaker, less developed member countries. This may very well amount to a setting in which the relative gainers are unable to compensate the relative losers "sufficiently" unless they give up virtually all their gains.

Similar considerations apply to integration among partners with a similar level of development and similar resource endowments such as the CACM or CARICOM. In such regional groupings there is little scope for interindustry specialisation since member countries tend to possess comparative advantages in the same products. Given the relatively low level of development, intraindustry specialisation does not offer an option either. Therefore, gains from integration are likely to remain low and uncertain as it is difficult to foresee in which way the regional pattern of production may be altered. Member countries which lose locational advantages in the production of certain products cannot be sure to be compensated by becoming attractive for other industries. Integration is, therefore, carried out in a slow and, more importantly, selective fashion which further reduces the gains emerging from trade concessions. In the end, there is very little incentive to continue to grant preferences or to pay compensation.

IV. Politico-Economic Reasons

1. The Political Economy of International Coordination

The above assessment of potential and actual gains from RIDC points to politico-economic aspects of integration and cooperation efforts. If governments can be assumed to behave rationally, they will cooperate with other countries in such a way as to maximise the utility of their own countries. The implications of this assumption for economic coordination among independent nations have been elaborated in the theory of clubs [as summarised in Fratianni, Pattison, 1982]. This reasoning applies to the case of RIDC as a special form of international coordination which allows to implement the exclusion principle, i.e. concessions can be restricted to member countries. For the membership in such clubs the following considerations are valid:

- Each country assesses the individual benefits and costs of the membership in a regional grouping. Decisions are made on the basis of the country's net benefits, and not on the basis of benefits achieved by the integration scheme as a whole.

- The larger the number of members in an integration scheme, the lower is the marginal benefit derived from an additional member for each of the old members.

- Membership costs are not equal for all members. In particular, addition of a new member will raise the costs of finding agreement, e.g. on preferential tariffs, in a more than proportionate manner since decisions have to reflect both the interests of old and of new members. Hence, finding agreement grows more costly with an increasing number of members, or excluding a marginal member may increase net benefits of the integration scheme derived by the remaining members.

- Governments tend to focus on financial flows rather than on total economic benefits and costs, when deciding on membership. Compensation payments or loss of government revenues as consequences of economic integration lend themselves much easier to a public demonstration of benefits and costs associated with membership than potential net gains from specialisation. Therefore, politicians prefer to argue on the basis of visible flows.

Judged by these criteria the crisis of RIDC appears in a different perspective. Lacking implementation of integration policies, new barriers to trade or exit from integration schemes were not so much cases of policy failure but rather the result of a rational economic calculus by governments of member countries. This is most obvious for countries which left customs unions such as Chad (CACEU), Benin (WAEC), Tanzania (EAC) or Honduras (CACM). To cancel membership was preferable because

- individual cost-benefit comparisons on the basis of visible flows had turned out to be negative,

- they had to shoulder higher costs than other members of the customs union and they were not able to win sufficient special concessions from other members to lower these costs,

- leading members of the respective customs unions did not consider their membership as beneficial enough for themselves to offer sufficient compensation payments.

The political economy of international coordination does also provide an explanation for other phenomena observed in the context of RIDC such as external cooperation without integration or the recent trends towards bilateralism. The advantage of bilateralism is obvious since two in general more advanced countries, such as Argentina and Brazil, with a different pattern of specialisation, can more easily find areas of common interest for partial deregulation. Selective trade liberalisation for specific products can provide access to new markets in the neighbouring country without generating adjustment pressures for other internationally not competitive industries.

External cooperation of regional groupings against an actual or perceived common threat (ASEAN, SADCC) is beneficial to member countries since they are jointly more successful in acquiring advantages than they would be on their own. Such advantages can take the form of political protection and military security (ASEAN) or they may materialise in an increased flow of development aid (SADCC). Net benefits are maximised when member countries minimise the costs of cooperation once external support has been secured. Although foreign support is tied to e.g. development projects or military spending, there are various avenues to reduce the costs of cooperation by avoiding economic integration. Thanks to the fungibility of funds governments can use their own resources in a way detrimental to integration: integration can be narrowed down to some marginal areas of common interest which then amounts to economic cooperation in some selected areas; or governments may simply not implement deregulation policies required for a free movement of goods and factors of production within the regional grouping.

2. Vested Interests

Underneath the political economy of international coordination there is a second (more microeconomic) layer of politico-economic influences on government decision making. Governments are either subject to the pressure of strong interest groups which oppose liberalisation that would expose inefficient import substitution activities to foreign competition. Or politicians and bureaucrats themselves may benefit from import substitution policies through their stake in inefficient public or private enterprises or their control over NTBs such as import quotas, licences, and foreign exchange allocations. Rationing allows them to make profits from illegal sales and corruption. The subordination of government decisions under individual welfare considerations has manifested itself in the dependence of politicians on influential businessmen in Latin America [e.g. Morawetz, 1981, pp. 98-99, 156-157] and the "personal rule" of parasitic elites in Africa [Bates, 1981; 1983; Jackson, Rosberg, 1982, p. 84; Sandbrook, 1985; 1986] or the emergence of a nonproductive state class living on rents [Elsenhans, 1984]. Vested interests in Africa further emerge from the competition among ethnical groups for political power and economic influence within individual countries that has resulted in the adoption of restrictions on firms that could benefit from trade liberalisation, e.g. in ECOWAS and the PTA.

The history of RIDC provides ample evidence for the influence of vested interests on the failure of integration efforts. Under inward-oriented trade regimes, many multinational companies have invested in neighbouring countries to supply domestic markets and earned the rents to be derived from protectionism. Those companies are not interested in trade liberalisation and will put pressure on government officials to prevent a change of the trade regime. Such pressure can be brought to bear particularly in many small African countries with only few major foreign investors [Robson, 1985, p. 615]. Such an example is the Bata shoe manufacturer which has subsidiaries in Benin, Burkina Faso, Cameroon, Central African Republic, Congo, Ivory Coast, Mauritania, Senegal, and Togo [Ediafric, 1987]. Another example concerns the production of aluminium household utensils by a French multinational in West and Central African countries [Agarwal et al., 1985, p. 103]. Similar patterns characterise the production of textiles and bicycles. Trade liberalisation among members of WAEC and CACEU would inevitably render some of these subsidiaries obsolete and is likely to reduce overall profits since production would have to be relocated to the least protectionist country.

The unwillingness to rely on the private sector in many African countries [Nellis, 1986] has led to the establishment of a few large public enterprises dominating the industrial sector. The destiny of these enterprises is often intimately intertwined with the interests of politicians and bureaucrats who seek to protect state enterprises by maintaining or even erecting new trade barriers contrary to the principles of integra-

72

tion they themselves had agreed to. Incidence for such a collusion of interests can be found in the penetration of public enterprises by government officials as was the case with military men usurping the commanding heights of public and semipublic companies in Nigeria [Berg-stresser, 1988].

F. Agenda for Policy Action

I. Promoting Cooperation and not Integration

The summary of experiences with RIDC presented in the preceding chapter is not encouraging. Viewed against the initial intentions to promote economic and social development by providing a training ground for infant economies, RIDC has more or less failed [cf. also Inotai, 1986, pp. 222 f.]. Regional trade did not offer a viable alternative to trade with industrialised countries and could not offset the disadvantages of an excessive import substitution policy applied in most member countries of regional groupings. Vested interests at the micro level as well as the meagre gains from such trade for the countries concerned soon discouraged further integration efforts or even led to a reversal of trade liberalisation and joint investment planning. Economic integration continued to be advocated in political fora, but has lost any influence on actual policy making for at least 15 years. The almost total dissatisfaction with regional trade liberalisation is growing out of the observation that virtually no success case can be cited in which this approach itself was instrumental in enhancing development processes in member countries. Even in ASEAN countries economic prosperity was rather derived from domestic policy reform than from regional integration.

For the purpose of policy conclusions, it is important to stress that the dismal results of RIDC did not so much result from a misperception of the potential embodied in regional trade integration, but from the lack of incentives to implement integration policies in the given situation. It has turned out that RIDC cannot be a substitute for appropriate domestic economic policies. With wrong exchange rates, high barriers to trade, misleading investment incentives, and a high degree of government participation in economic activities, patterns of production and trade are distorted in such a way that economic integration does not offer many benefits to those gaining from the domestic economic policy regime. Therefore, they oppose regional economic liberalisation as much as they oppose opening up towards world markets. This opposition could not be overruled since politicians either have direct vested interests in distorted patterns of production and trade (Africa) or private pressure groups command sufficient resources to influence government decisions (Latin

America).

Compensation payments do not open a way out of this politico-economic stalemate either. Regional import substitution as a substitute for national import substitution does not produce significant gains from trade or factor mobility especially if the majority of the regional counterparts is economically weak. Immediate losses of government revenues as well as employment and output in obsolete industries in weak partner countries create a demand for compensation which is not met by the more advanced countries expecting relatively low and often uncertain medium term gains. To remedy this situation by replenishing compensation funds from external (bilateral or multilateral) sources is hardly an option for several reasons. Given the difficulties of assessing the amount and duration of economically justified compensation, developmental considerations are likely to be substituted by a political bargaining process. The question then is who is being paid for what, i. e. the purpose of disbursing external funds becomes unclear, and more advanced member countries may easily feel to be at a disadvantage since they do not benefit from similar support. And finally, compensation payments required to break the opposition of vested interests may be out of proportion compared to the envisaged benefits from integration. This casts doubt on the developmental impact of external funds used for this purpose and may also become questionable from a distributional point of view.

The bottomline of the experiences with RIDC is that economic integration in the traditional sense (customs unions, common markets, joint investment planning) has proven not to be viable. There seems to be no alternative to trade liberalisation on a nondiscriminatory basis. What remains are scattered examples of regional cooperation in specific areas of common interest among partner countries. Such common interests were found in the dealing with actual or perceived external threats or in the joint production of public goods (education, research and development (R&D), infrastructure, environment) which would have been too costly for individual countries (ASEAN, GCC, SADCC, ECOWAS). Turning from the past to the future, the latter appears to offer the only starting point for a promotion of RIDC. Human resource development, food security, expansion of R&D especially in agriculture, energy management, environment problems, international marketing and improved flows of information and communication represent severe bottlenecks to economic development, particularly in the poorer countries of Africa and Central America, which could be widened by intraregional cooperation. By its very nature, this type of cooperation will, however, be very selective and country-specific. It will not lend itself to large-scale aid projects, but rather have to focus on the provision of "software" such as the design of appropriate joint policies of partner countries and the establishment of joint management or control facilities. "Hardware" requirements such as infrastructure or equipment should be derived from software-oriented projects and programmes and not be anticipated as independent tasks because all efforts towards a joint provision of railway links, energy supply and other infrastructure have been fraught with almost unsurmountable financing and management difficulties.

The success of regional cooperation in lieu of integration hinges on several preconditions. Firstly, the initiative for cooperation has to come from within the countries concerned. Frequently aborted IMF (International Monetary Fund) and World Bank adjustment programmes have proven that an appropriate macro and sector policy management cannot be imposed externally. The same applies even more to regional cooperation. The strategic policy changes towards encouraging cooperation have to emerge from the desire of the countries themselves to engage in a partnership with external donors mainly playing a catalytic role. Except for technical assistance in policy analysis and policy implementation, there are fewer external donors which could directly contribute to setting the wheel in motion.

The second prerequisite for successful regional cooperation is domestic policy reform in the participating countries. As long as misguided incentive systems distort the pattern of production and trade, there is also not much scope for successful regional cooperation. Empirical evidence of the past three decades has clearly highlighted the importance of a stable macroeconomic environment, i.e. stable monetary and fiscal policies, and the critical role of prices, in particular the exchange rate, for economic development. Unless governments reduce their role to providing an appropriate economic framework for the initiatives of individual economic agents, i.e. farmers, entrepreneurs and traders, gains from regional cooperation are easily foregone because it is difficult to detect promising areas for cooperation in a highly distorted environment and because the joint production of public goods will not be met by the necessary response of private agents. This response is required, however, if cooperation among governments is to be translated into more production and employment.

Finally, regional cooperation should not be discouraged by the external economic environment that participating countries are facing. If cooperation is to be successful in the sense that diversification into new economic activities and a division of labour among partner countries are promoted it is the task of OECD countries to provide unrestricted access to their markets for products originating from regional groupings. This precondition seems to be fulfilled given the far-reaching special and general preferences for low-income countries (Lomé Agreement, Caribbean Basin Initiative, GSP), but some subtle protectionist remnants are still embodied in preferential trading arrangements that discriminate in particular against an intraregional division of labour as will be discussed below.

II. The Potential Contributions of Bilateral and Multilateral Donors

1. Review of OECD Countries' Policies

To provide access to all OECD markets and to secure an uninterrupted availability of imports is an essential and indispensable part of OECD support for economic development in Third World countries in general [Hiemenz, 1989]. What matters in the context of regional cooperation are, firstly, agricultural protectionism in OECD countries and the associated distribution of surplus production in the form of food aid which discourage joint food security policies on a regional level. Artificially lowered world market prices and policy-induced price instabilities[1] constitute disincentives for local agricultural production and raise the market risk of developing countries in food trade.

Secondly, protectionist instruments embodied in preferential trading arrangements are subtle but by no means ineffective since they have discouraged efforts to establish internationally competitive lines of pro-

---

[1] Anderson, Tyres [1986]; Tyers, Anderson [1988, pp. 285 f.]; Valdés, Zietz [1980].

duction and nourished export pessimism of potential investors, above all in economically weak countries.[1] In particular, rules of origin are too restrictive given the stage of industrialisation in economically weak countries. They prevent these countries not only from attracting "finishing touch" activities which can be a first step towards developing an indigenous industrial sector, but also from engaging in a vertical division of labour among regional partner countries.[2]

2. Support for Domestic Policy Reform

As elaborated above domestic policy reform will greatly improve the scope for and the gains from economic cooperation. Structural adjustment loans granted under the auspices of IMF and World Bank have supported domestic policy reforms in the past, but these efforts have met severe constraints, and the final outcome is highly uncertain in many cases [World Bank, 1988a; 1988b, p. 28]. There are at least two major reasons for the lagging progress with policy reform in many developing countries suffering from severe policy-induced distortions. Firstly, empirical evidence suggests that external financial support for governments under-taking economic reforms has lagged behind their needs in the past [Gulhati, Nallari, 1988]. According to this evidence, it was at least partly due to lacking aid response, particularly by bilateral donors, that policy reforms were abandoned or stagnated in several African countries such as Malawi, Zaire, Zambia, and Uganda. A reward of reform efforts will, of course, require the specification of criteria upon which aid disbursements can be based.

And secondly, as politico-economic constraints and institutional weaknesses were identified as major bottlenecks for development in many countries, external assistance may have to focus on rather fundamental issues before a successful policy reform can be implemented. In countries

---

[1] Agarwal et al. [1985, Section IV]; McQueen [1982]; McQueen, Yannopoulos [1989].

[2] The EC has introduced cumulative rules of origin for three regional groupings (CACM, ASEAN, Andean Group) in its GSP, but only for a limited range of products and under restrictive conditions.

characterised by strong vested interests development aid should be
geared towards institution building, human resource development, control
of population growth and other poverty-related areas [Hiemenz, 1989].
This "software" orientation deserves much greater attention in the future
design of aid programmes since it will not only pave the way to domestic
policy reform, but also facilitate the political economy of economic cooperation.

3. Support for Economic Cooperation

The preceding section has highlighted a number of areas suited for
economic cooperation among developing countries which would fit into
domestic policy reform programmes. Given the politico-economic constraints for policy making in these countries that have been elaborated
above, the desire for cooperation will emerge only in cases when cooperation serves mutual interests, i.e. when participating countries
stand to gain from cooperation in a similar manner and vested interests
can be overruled or compensated. These preconditions will, if at all, be
met in the joint production of public goods. The fact that a large number of such cooperation projects have already been implemented with
external support bears witness to this point. To encourage the design
and implementation of further projects and programmes the following
provides an overview of principal avenues to economic cooperation in the
production of public goods.

Government policies and public institutions provide a framework for
the activities of individual economic agents, and hence, there is scope
for cooperation in almost any market or sector of the economy. Cooperation is likely to be most desirable and effective in the deregulation and
development of factor markets such as labour and capital markets or
science and technology, as well as in the design and implementation of
fiscal policies. Particularly in countries at an early stage of development,
there may also be great benefits to be gained from cooperation at the
sectoral level with respect to policies and institutions pertaining to food,
agriculture and forestry, industry, minerals and energy, or trade,
transport and communication. Concerning the type of cooperation a hier-
archical order is discernible depending on the loss of autonomous de-

cision making required by cooperation. The possibilities stretch from a mere exchange of information via the provision of joint training facilities and via a mutual recognition and adaptation of rules and regulations to the implementation of joint policies and, finally, the establishment of joint institutions with at least quasi-legislative power. In principal, all types of cooperations can be instituted in all areas of mutual interest among participating countries.

An improved flow of information is almost inevitably a necessary first step to lay the groundwork for economic cooperation. Institution-alised access to information on rules and regulations implemented in partner countries and on bureaucratic procedures such as customs and tax administration, public procurement, or the evaluation of investment applications will help bureaucrats and businessmen to assess the obstac-les against and the potential for an expansion of economic activities across borders. A timely publication of standardised statistical data is another aspect of this type of cooperation, which may also require an improvement of technical facilities available in administrations such as computerisation. In addition, efforts can be undertaken to share infor-mation on the external economic environment among partner countries. There may be a joint interest in technologies, markets, barriers to trade, and marketing channels in industrialised countries, and it may be efficient to obtain this information jointly. If the perceived benefits of pursuing a cooperative information policy are large enough, partner countries may choose to go all the way to establishing common infor-mation centres.

The lack of human capital generally constitutes a major bottleneck to economic development. Both appropriate policy formulation and effi-cient private decision making require a well-trained technocratic elite, the emergence of which could be accelerated if countries cooperate in training. There are many important subjects such as modern techniques of government administration, the adaptation of Western technologies, the functioning of labour and capital markets, and international trade and marketing which may be suitable for joint training of senior administra-tive staff and private entrepreneurs. The options for joint training range from study tours and courses in existing institutions to the estab-lishment of specialised joint training centres. They do also include the development of curricula and teaching material.

The cooperation projects discussed so far must be classified as borderline cases of the production of public goods. In economically more advanced countries such services may be supplied more efficiently by the private sector. Therefore, an evaluation of these projects has to include an assessment of the competition between public and private suppliers of the respective services so as to prevent crowding-out of private suppliers by, generally subsidised, public institutions. Such a precaution does not have to be taken in joint efforts to improve the policy framework for more economic exchange among partner countries. In its weak form policy coordination may focus on streamlining and facilitating rules, regulations and norms, adjusting customs, tax and other administrative procedures, and mutual recognition of privileges or rights of access obtained in member countries. The aim is to achieve greater transparency of government intervention in markets and to standardise these interventions among partner countries as much as possible to remove barriers to access for people and goods.

A stronger form of policy coordination are joint policies which can be of mutual benefit when policy implications cannot be limited to the national economies. Potential candidates for such an approach are the joint exploitation of internationally mobile resources, joint energy and water management, environmental protection, control of population growth, food security, and surveillance of air and marine transport, fishing rights and trade in narcotics and weapons. This list is by no means exhaustive, but all joint policies have in common that mutual agreement has to be reached with respect to policy design and implementation. When decisions need to be made frequently, the establishment of joint institutions endowed with certain administrative powers may be preferable over tedious negotiations between government representatives. Hence, the borderline between joint policies and joint institutions is thin. Joint policies may be executed by surveillance bodies, agencies, or councils.

Another reason for establishing joint institutions is cost sharing. The size of domestic demand and/or budgetary considerations may suggest to pursue certain government activities on a cooperative basis with other partner countries. Cases in point are e.g. research and training centres for a wide range of mutually interesting subjects (agricultural development, industrial technologies, banking, marketing, energy, environmental issues, climate, health, nutrition).

In establishing such institutions, it is an important consideration that participating countries are extremely sensitive to an equal distribution of benefits derived from the activities of the institutions. Extended discussions about the best location for a new institution are but one sign of this sensitivity, and many joint institutions have stagnated or were even dissolved because individual member countries did not make their financial contributions or were dissatisfied with their benefits from cooperation. The design of new institutions would, therefore, require a careful assessment of the benefits derived by each individual member country and, possibly, the introduction of monitoring devices which increase the transparency of the distribution of costs and benefits. Furthermore, the functioning of institutions may require some forms of sanctions against member countries which fail to meet their commitments.

The overview of potential areas for successful cooperation among developing countries clearly indicates the supplementary nature of such efforts. Likewise, most cooperation projects or programmes are likely to be small in terms of the required external financial support. Improving the flow of information and policy coordination will in the first place be a matter of providing technical assistance. Foreign exchange requirements may arise in the context of rehabilitating existing institutions or creating new ones. In economically weaker countries, the absorptive capacity for such projects is however limited due to the scarcity of skilled personal. For these reasons, the main thrust of external assistance should be geared towards supporting domestic policy reform as outlined above.

Appendix Tables

Table A1 - Empirical Evidence for the "Training Ground" Argument - Rank Spearman Correlation Coefficients Between Absolute Growth of Intra- and Extraregional Exports of Manufactures

Integration scheme	Period	Aggregation level	Sample size	Correlation coefficient	Author (year)
CACM	1962-1968	5-digit SITC > US $ 50000	44	0.0826	Morawetz [1974]
CACM	1962-1968	ditto	40	0.2887	ditto
CACM	1962-1968	5-digit SITC	126	0.297*	Heldt [1976]
CACM	1968-1971	ditto	ditto	0.255*	ditto
CACM	Intraregional exports: 1962-1968 Extraregional exports: 1968-1971	n.a.	n.a.	0.555*	ditto
LAFTA	1962-1972	3-digit SITC	n.a.		ditto
Argentina				0.280	
Brazil				0.430*	
Chile				0.383	
Colombia				0.040	
Mexico				0.277	
Andean Group	1968-1972	ditto	n.a.		ditto
Chile				0.312	
Colombia				-0.412	
EAC	1964-1973	5-digit SITC (excl.67+68)			Langhammer [1976]
Kenya			52	0.15	
Tanzania			20	-0.07	
Uganda			5	0.33	
CACEU	1966-1971	ditto			ditto
Cameroon			26	-0.08	
Congo			7	-0.09	
CAR			8	0.22	
CUWAS	1966-1971	ditto			ditto
Ivory Coast			87	-0.15	
Senegal			98	-0.08	
Mauritania			33	-0.19	

*Statistically significant at the 1 per cent level. - n.a. = not available.

Table A2 - Multilateral Clearing and Payments Arrangements of Developing Countries, Main Operating Statistics, 1986-1988

	(1)	(2)	(3)	(4)	(5)
	Volume of transactions channelled through the arrangements	Transactions cleared	Transactions settled in foreign exchange	Share of (3) in (1) ((4)=(3)/(1))	Share of trans- actions in total intraregional trade
	mill. US $			per cent	
	Central American Clearing House				
1986	189.0	149.0	40.5	21.4	30.5
1987	210.5	165.0	45.5	21.6	n.a.
1988	98.0	64.0	34.0	34.7	n.a.
	LAIA Payments and Reciprocal Credit Systems				
1986	6268	5289.5	978.5	15.6	76.3
1987	6926	5719.0	1207.0	17.4	79.2
1988	9524	7207.0	2317.0	24.3	n.a.
	Asian Clearing Union				
1986	659.5	455.1	204.4	31.0	n.a.
1987	580.0	460.0	120.0	20.7	n.a.
1988(a)	217.0	165.0	52.0	24.0	n.a.
	West African Clearing House				
1986	109.3	15.4	93.9	85.9	22.3
1987	56.5	5.2	51.3	90.8	n.a.
1988(a)	26.2	6.1	20.1	76.7	n.a.
	PTA Clearing Arrangement				
1986	79.0	14.2	64.8	82.0	n.a.
1987	65.2	53.2	12.0	18.4	n.a.
1988(a)	64.0	33.0	31.0	48.4	n.a.

(a) First six months. - n.a. = not available.

Source: ALADI [b, 1989, No. 2]; UNCTAD [c].

84

Table A3 - Intra-Group Trade as a Percentage of Total Exports of
Selected Integration Schemes, 1970-1986

	1970	1980	1981	1982	1983	1984	1985	1986
Sub-Saharan Africa								
CACEU	3.4	4.1	3.0	3.6	2.0	4.1	2.0	2.8
ECOWAS	2.1	3.9	4.6	4.1	4.1	2.5	2.5	3.2
WAEC	9.1	6.9	10.1	10.7	11.6	7.4	7.1	6.5
Latin America								
LAIA	10.2	13.5	12.6	13.2	10.2	9.2	9.6	11.8
Andean Group	2.3	3.5	3.4	4.5	4.3	3.3	3.1	3.3
CACM	26.8	22.0	20.7	21.8	21.8	19.7	15.9	18.0
CARICOM	7.3	6.4	7.4	9.0	9.3	4.2	5.5	5.5
ASIA								
GCC	n.a.	3.0	n.a.	4.2	3.9	4.1	4.6	4.6
ECO	1.1	2.7	4.2	6.4	4.8	11.0	10.0	9.1
ASEAN	14.7	17.8	18.9	23.3	23.1	18.5	17.9	17.5
Bangkok Agreement	1.5	1.8	1.9	2.1	3.2	4.3	2.5	2.2

(a) Data for 1986 are provisional estimates compiled and computed by the UNCTAD Secretariat from information provided mainly by the Secretariats of integration groupings. Data for GCC countries are compiled from a report of the ESCWA Secretariat (E/ESCWA/DPD/87/21). - n.a. = not available.

Source: UNCTAD [a].

Synoptical Table A1 - Estimates on Trade Creation and Trade Diversion in RIDC, 1952-1979

Schemes	Authors	Methodology	Period	Results
LAFTA	George et al. [1977]	Estimates of demand functions for imports of individual LAFTA member and nonmember countries; integration dummies are used, trade effects are estimated as differences between actual and hypothetical imports	1952-1969	Intra-LAFTA trade expansion was mainly due to trade diversion; 75 per cent of estimated diversion was accounted for by Argentina: foreign exchange constraint appears as an important factor for intra-LAFTA trade
LAFTA	Aitken, Lowry [1973]	Cross-sectional bilateral trade flow model (gravity model); integration dummies	1955-1967	Gross trade creation defined as total increase in intra-LAFTA trade is found to be relevant; no significant trade diversion
LAFTA	Langhammer, Spinanger [1984, pp. 57-63]	Trade diversion measured as difference between absolute changes in actual intra-LAFTA imports and those changes which would have occurred under constant share of intra-LAFTA imports in total imports; thirty three-digit SITC groups	1962-1979	Trade diversion accounts for the largest part of growth of imports of Mexico; Brazil and Argentina from LAFTA members
CACM	Wilford [1970]	Balassa approach: comparison of pre- and post-integration ex post income elasticities of import demand	1956-1967	Net trade creation after the foundation of the CACM = increase in the income elasticity of import demand for total imports
CACM	Aitken, Lowry [1973]	Cross-sectional bilateral trade flow model (gravity model); integration dummies	1955-1967	Gross trade creation increased progressively after 1961; no significant trade diversion
CACM	Willmore [1976]	Balassa approach (see above) for durable and nondurable consumer goods and intermediate goods	1958-1968	Trade diversion in nondurable consumer goods; external trade creation in intermediate goods; no conclusive results for durables
CACEU	Langhammer [1978, pp. 76-80]	Net trade creation is measured as growth of share of intraregional imports in total domestic supply minus decrease of share of extraregional imports; trade diversion is defined as extraregional import substitution fully compensated by growth of intra-regional imports	1966-1970	Extraregional imports were replaced more by domestic production than by intraregional imports; trade creation was negligible

Synoptical Table A2 - Summary Records of Summit Meetings of Major Sub-Saharan African Integration Schemes, 1985-1988

Venue	Participation (Heads of State)	Problems stated	Decisions taken
Summary Record 1985-1988 of Summit Meetings of the WAEC			
26-27 March 1986 Ouagadougou	Complete, Guinea and Togo as observers	Lack of financial controls; absence of viable management in the overstaffed Secretariat; no agreement on management report; far-reaching corruption problems	Adoption of new regional projects for commercial information and documentation, and for solar energy; budget of the "Solidarity and Intervention Fund for the Development of the Community" adopted; no decision on integration deepening
21-22 April 1987 Nouakchott	Incomplete, Senegal and Niger missing	Distribution conflicts between Senegal and Ivory Coast on one hand and Burkina Faso, Niger and Mali on the other hand; introduction of new barriers (transit tax by Burkina Faso; import ban on cotton and fruit)	Solidarity Fund is placed directly under the authority of the Secretariat instead of the acting president of the Council of Ministers; cut of the operational budget by 10 per cent
No summit meeting in 1988			By 1989, a Community levy to ensure the regional organisation's own and permanent income is to come into force

Members: Benin, Burkina Faso, Ivory Coast, Mali, Mauritania, Niger, and Senegal.

Venue	Participation (Heads of State)	Problems stated	Decisions taken
Summary Record 1985-1988 of Summit Meetings of the PTA			
18 December 1985 Lusaka	Incomplete, Comoros, Djibouti, Ethiopia, Kenya, Lesotho, Malawi, Mauritius, Rwanda, Somalia, Swaziland, and Uganda were	Clearing house at the Reserve Bank of Zimbabwe to maximise local currency trade was used by only six members and handled only 4 per cent of total intra-	Discussion on reduction and standardisation of tariffs on a common list postponed; reduction of local ownership requirement for rules of origin

Synoptical Table A2 continued

Venue	Participation (Heads of State)	Problems stated	Decisions taken
	missing. Potential members Angola, Botswana, Mocambique, Madagascar, and Seychelles sent observers	regional trade; rules of origin stipulating that exports eligible for preferences must come from businesses at least 51 per cent locally owned were argued to be too restrictive; payments arrears	to 30 per cent discussed
27-28 May 1986 Bujumbura (extra-ordinary Summit)	Incomplete, only Kenya, Uganda, Zambia and Zimbabwe, and Burundi were present	PTA Development Bank membership not attractive; Mauritius left the PTA; payments arrears	Three-tier system approved: 100 per cent preferential treatment for companies with minimum 51 per cent local equity holding, 60 per cent for companies between 41 and 50 per cent; 90 per cent for companies between 30 and 40 per cent local equity; schedules for "common list" approved
3-4 December 1987 Kampala	Incomplete, five out of 15 heads of state were present	Clearing house still insufficiently used by member countries	Schedule for intraregional trade liberalisation approved: 10 per cent reduction annually between 1988-1996; introduction of travellers' cheques in PTA Currency Units (PTACU) to ease commercial exchanges and to set businessmen free from the current restrictions; community sanctions against South Africa deferred
25 May 1988 Addis Ababa	Incomplete, eight heads of state were		PTA traveller cheques to be introduced 1 August 1988, com-

Synoptical Table A2 continued

Venue	Participation (Heads of State)	Problems stated	Decisions taken
	present		pulsory for all travellers within the area; sweeping sanctions against South Africa launched
Members: Botswana, Burundi, Comoros, Ethiopia, Kenya, Lesotho, Malawi, Mauritius, Rwanda, Somalia, Swaziland, Tanzania, Uganda, Zambia, Zimbabwe			
Summary Record of 1985-1988 of Summit Meetings of the ECCAS			
23-24 January 1986 Yaounde	Incomplete, CAR were missing	Budget contributions of member states (arrears); free circulation of persons in the ECCAS controversially discussed	Programme of action approved
28 August 1987 Libreville	Incomplete, Burundi, CAR, Chad, Rwanda, Sao Tomé and Principe, Zaire were missing	See above	Budget approved for 1987; organisation for a trade fair in Kinshasa in 1989 approved
26-27 February 1988 Kinshasa	Complete	See above; only four out of the ten members had paid up	Clearing house foundation has been given "top priority"
Members: Burundi, Cameroon, CAR, Chad, Congo, Gabon, Equatorial Guinea, Rwanda, Sao Tomé and Principe, Zaire			
Summary Record 1985-1988 of the Summit Meetings of the CACEU			
19 December 1985 Souba/Gabon	Complete	Free circulation of goods and services still under scrutiny; free movement of labour not agreed upon by Cameroon and Gabon	No relevant decision taken

Synoptical Table A2 continued

89

Venue	Participation (Heads of State)	Problems stated	Decisions taken
19 December 1987 N'Djamena	Incomplete, Cameroon, Congo and CAR were missing (informal meeting on 8 January 1988)	Precarious financial situation of the Central African States' Bank; no agreement launched on free circulation of persons within the region	Meeting approved a budget for 1988 down 22 per cent. No relevant decision taken with three of six heads absent
December 1988 Yaounde	No information		

Members: Cameroon, Chad, Congo, CAR, Gabon, Equatorial Guinea

Summary Record 1985-1988 of the Summit Meetings of the ECOWAS

Venue	Participation (Heads of State)	Problems stated	Decisions taken
6 July 1985 Lomé	Incomplete, Ghana, Mauritania, Cape Verde, and Guinea-Bissau were missing	Illegal immigrants expelled from Nigeria violates Phase II of the 1979 immigration protocol which allows ECOWAS citizens unlimited residence in member states as from 1985; implementation of the protocol postponed until the 1986 summit	Adoption of a plan to build new headquarters for the ECOWAS Secretariat and the ECOWAS Fund for Cooperation; setting up of a regional bank with 20 per cent equity participation of ECOWAS members; ECOWAS telecommunication project proceeds
30 June - 2 July 1986 Abuja	Incomplete, Niger, Mali, Guinea, Ghana, Ivory Coast were missing	Arrears cumulated up to twice the annual budget; telecommunication link-up project delayed because of finanical shortages. No decision taken on the economic recovery programme adopted at the Lomé Summit; bilateral border conflicts; trade liberalisation remains a "dormant" problematic issue; adopted provisions have not been implemented	Adoption of the "beginning of the implementation of Phase II of the protocol on free movement of people"

Synoptical Table A2 continued

Venue	Participation (Heads of State)	Problems stated	Decisions taken
7 July 1987 Abuja	Incomplete, Ghana, Niger, Guinea-Bissau, Senegal, Guinea, Sierra Leone and Liberia, and Mauritania were missing	No information	Launching of the ECOWAS Recovery Programme (money needed is to be raised outside ECOWAS; volume US $ 926 mill.); summit confirmed the authorised capital of ECOWAS Fund as US $ 500 mill.; setting up of a West African Health organisation
24-25 June 1988 Lomé	Incomplete, Guinea	No progress of trade liberalisation; arrears remain unsettled	Opening of the ECOWAS Fund to nonregional countries and institutions, cooperation agreement with the African Development Bank, cooperation start with the World Bank; no dumping of toxic and nuclear waste in the region.

Summary Record of 1985-1988 of Summit Meetings of the SADCC

Members: Benin, Burkina Faso, Cape Verde, Ivory Coast, Gambia, Ghana, Guinea, Guinea-Bissau, Liberia, Mali, Mauritania, Niger, Nigeria, Senegal, Sierra Leone, Togo

Venue	Participation (Heads of State)	Problems stated	Decisions taken
9 August 1985 Arusha	Incomplete, Malawi and Swaziland were missing	Disparity within SADCC towards sanctions against South Africa	No information
21-22 August 1986 Luanda	Incomplete, Malawi, Swaziland, and Lesotho were missing	See above	No information

Synoptical Table A2 continued

Venue	Participation (Heads of State)	Problems stated	Decisions taken
24 July 1987 Lusaka	Incomplete, Malawi and Swaziland were missing	See above, declining economic prospects	US $ 2500 mill. secured from both local and foreign contribution for the SADCC's US $ 6000 mill. programme of action (rehabilitation and improvement of transport links to region's main ports of Maputo, Beira, Nacala, Dar-es-Salam, and Lobito); establishment of SADCC Business Councils discussed; study on harmonisation of investment codes to be commissioned
15 July 1988 Maputo	No information	See above	Botswana provides aid for the rehabilitation of the Limpopo railway
MEMO: 28-29 January 1988 Consultative Meeting with donors in Arusha	No information	Unwillingness of Canada, Australia and other donors to cede control over food to support SADCC's proposed US $ 208 mill. food reserve project; concern of donors over Zimbabwe's proposed extension of energy supply from the Kariba South hydroelectric station despite the availability of surplus electricity from the Zambian side of the scheme	Fund raising of roughly US $ 1 bill. over the 1988-1991 period mainly for the transport and communication sector. Donors: EC members, Nordic countries, Canada, Australia; the US discuss the creation of an export pre-financing revolving fund to overcome foreign exchange constraints in Angola, Malawi, Mocambique and Zambia; support pledged by some donors for the Limpopo railway rehabilitation project

Members: Angola, Botswana, Lesotho, Malawi, Mocambique, Swaziland, Tanzania, Zambia, Zimbabwe

Synoptical Table A2 continued

Summary Record of 1985-1987 of Summit Meetings of the Senegal River Development Organisation

Venue	Participation (Heads of State)	Problems stated	Foreign aid received	Decisions taken
25-26 March 1985 Nouakchott	Complete	Serious financial difficulties on the Manantali Dam; Kuwait blocked credit payments due to nonpayment of interest by Mali and Mauritania	French development aid agency open up credits for a total of 26 mill. FF for Manantali	No information
26-27 October 1987 Bamako	Complete	Disagreement between Senegal and Mauritania on the route of electricity lines serving the two countries from the Mali-based Manantali Dam; (disagreement in principle settled); aid donors reluctant to give priority to the navigation phase of the Diama and Manantali projects over production of energy and irrigation		River navigation - third phase of the river development programme - has been given political priority

Members: Mali, Mauritania, Sengal

Source: Africa Research Bulletin [various issues].

Bibliography

AFRICA RESEARCH BULLETIN, Economic Series. London, various issues.

AGARWAL, Jamuna P., Martin DIPPL, Rolf J. LANGHAMMER, EC Trade Policies Towards Associated Developing Countries. Barriers to Success. Kieler Studien, 193, Tübingen 1985.

AITKEN, Norman D., William R. LOWRY, "A Cross-Sectional Study of the Effects of LAFTA and CACM on Latin American Trade". Journal of Common Market Studies, Vol. 12, 1973, pp. 326-336.

AKANO, Olasupo, "Trade Statistics in ECOWAS: Problems and Needs". In: Adeyinka ORIMALADE, R.E. UBOGU (Eds.), Trade and Development in Economic Community of West African States (ECOWAS). New Delhi 1984, pp. 183-198.

AKINYEMI, A. Bolagi, S.B. FALEGAN, J.A. ALUKO (Eds.), Readings and Documents on ECOWAS. Lagos 1984.

ALADI [a], Newsletter. Montevideo, current issues.

-- [b], Sintesis. Montevideo, current issues.

ANDERSON, Kym, Rodney TYERS, "Agricultural Policies of Industrial Countries and their Effects on Traditional Food Exporters". The Economic Record, Vol. 62, 1986, pp. 385-399.

ANDIC, Fuat M., Suphan ANDIC, Douglas DOSSER, A Theory of Economic Integration for Developing Countries. London 1971.

ANJARIA, Shailendra J., Sena EKEN, John F. LAKER, Payments Arrangements and the Expansion of Trade in Eastern and Southern Africa. IMF, Occasional Paper No. 11, Washington, D.C., July 1982.

ASANTE, S.K.B., "ECOWAS/CEAO: Conflict and Cooperation in West Africa". In: Ralph I. ONWUKA, Amadu SESAY (Eds.), The Future of Regionalism in Africa. New York 1985, pp. 74-95.

--, The Political Economy of Regionalism in Africa. A Decade of the Economic Community of West African States (ECOWAS). New York 1986.

ASEAN [1987a], The Tasks Ahead. Institute of Southeast Asian Studies, Singapore 1987.

-- [1987b], The Way Forward. The Report of the Group of Fourteen on ASEAN Economic Co-operation and Integration. Institute of Strategic and International Studies, Kuala Lumpur 1987.

ASEAN Secretariat, Annual Report of the ASEAN Standing Committee, 1987-1988. Jakarta 1988.

BAHADIR, Sefik Alp, Theorien und Strategien der regionalen Wirtschaftsintegration von Entwicklungsländern. Berlin 1984.

BALASSA, Bela, The Theory of Economic Integration. London 1962.

--, "Regional Integration of Trade: Policies of Less Developed Countries". In: Paul STREETEN (Ed.), Trade Strategies for Development. New York 1973, pp. 176-186.

--, "Types of Economic Integration". In: Fritz MACHLUP (Ed.), Economic Integration: Worldwide, Regional, Sectoral. Proceedings of the 4th Congress of the International Economic Association held in Budapest. London 1976, pp. 17-31.

--, "Intra-Industry Trade and the Integration of Developing Countries in the World Economy". In: Herbert GIERSCH (Ed.), On the Economics of Intra-Industry Trade. Symposium 1978. Tübingen 1979, pp. 245-270.

BATES, Robert H., Markets and States in Tropical Africa. The Political Basis of Agricultural Policies. Berkeley 1981.

--, Essays on the Political Economy of Rural Africa. Cambridge, Mass., 1983.

BERGSTRESSER, Heinrich, "Wirtschaft und Politik in Nigeria". Afrikaspektrum, Vol. 2, 1988, pp. 183-200.

BLEJER, Mario I., Regional Integration in Latin America: The Experience and the Outlook for Further Cooperation. Paper presented at the Armand HAMMER Conference on Economic Cooperation in the Middle East. Tel Aviv University, Tel Aviv, April 1986 (mimeo).

BRADA, Josef C., José A. MENDEZ, "Regional Economic Integration and the Volume of Intra-Regional Trade: A Comparison of Developed and Developing Country Experience". Kyklos, Vol. 36, 1983, pp. 589-603.

BREWSTER, Havelock, Industrial Integration Systems. UNCTAD-Document TD/B/345, New York, 7 July 1971.

CARNOY, Martin, Industrialization in a Latin American Common Market. Washington, D.C., 1972.

CHNG Meng Kng, "ASEAN Economic Co-operation: The Current Status". Institute of Southeast Asian Studies (Ed.), Southeast Asian Affairs 1985. Singapore 1985, pp. 31-53.

COOPER, Charles A., Benton F. MASSELL, "Towards a General Theory of Customs Unions for Developing Countries". Journal of Political Economy, Vol. 73, 1965, pp. 461-476.

DEARDORFF, Alan V., Wolfgang F. STOLPER, "Effects of Smuggling under African Conditions: A Factual, Institutional and Analytic Discussion". Weltwirtschaftliches Archiv, Vol. 126, 1990, pp. 116-141.

DEVARAJAN, Shantayanan, Jaime de MELO, "Adjustment with a Fixed Exchange Rate: Cameroon, Côte d'Ivoire, and Senegal". The World Bank Economic Review, Vol. 1, 1987, pp. 447-487.

EDIAFRIC (Ed.), L'Annuaire des Societés et Fournisseurs. Vol. 2, L'Annuaire d'Afrique Noire 1986/87. Paris 1987.

EKWE, Victor, "Vérification des Entreprises Soumises au Regime de la Taxe Unique". Le Défi, No. 13, Bangui, July 1987, p. 81.

ELSENHANS, Hartmut, Abhängiger Kapitalismus oder bürokratische Entwicklungsgesellschaft. Versuch über den Staat in der Dritten Welt. Frankfurt 1984.

FISCHER, Bernhard, "Finanzielle Zusammenarbeit zwischen den Entwicklungsländern". Die Weltwirtschaft, 1983, No. 1, pp. 160-176.

FODERS, Federico, Handelspolitik und weltwirtschaftliche Integration von Entwicklungsländern. Das Beispiel Argentiniens, Brasiliens und Jamaikas. München 1987.

FRATIANNI, Michèle, John PATTISON, "The Economics of International Organizations". Kyklos, Vol. 35, 1982, pp. 244-262.

GEHRELS, Franz, "Customs Union from a Single-Country View-Point". Review of Economic Studies, Vol. 24, 1956/57, pp. 61-64.

GEORGE, Robert, Eldon REILING, Anthony SCAPERLANDA, "Short-Run Trade Effects of the LAFTA". Kyklos, Vol. 30, 1977, pp. 618-636.

GRANBERG, Per, Some Estimates of Intra-PTA Trade. DERAP Working Papers, No. A 350, Bergen, December 1985.

GULHATI, Ravi, Raji NALLARI, "Reform of Foreign Aid Policies: The Issue of Inter-Country Allocation in Africa". World Development, Vol. 16, 1988, pp. 1167-1184.

HALDI, John, David WHITCOMB, "Economies of Scale in Industrial Plants". The Journal of Political Economy, Vol. 75, 1967, pp. 373-385.

HAY, Roger W., Mandivamba RUKUNI, "SADCC Food Security Strategies. Evolution and Role". World Development, Vol. 16, 1988, pp. 1013-1024.

HAZLEWOOD, Arthur, Economic Integration: The East African Experience. London 1975.

--, "The End of the East African Community: What are the Lessons for Regional Integration Schemes?". Journal of Common Market Studies, Vol. 18, 1979, pp. 40-58.

HELDT, Sven, The Andean Group: An Answer to Some Problems of LAFTA. Institute für Weltwirtschaft, Kiel Discussion Papers, 18, February 1972.

--, Zur Messung von Integrationseffekten im Zentralamerikanischen Gemeinsamen Markt. Institut für Weltwirtschaft, Kiel Working Papers, 19, June 1974.

--, "Regionale Integration zwischen lateinamerikanischen Staaten als Vorbedingung für Industriewarenexporte nach Drittländern?". Die Weltwirtschaft, 1976, No. 1, pp. 117-131.

HIEMENZ, Ulrich, Development Strategies and Foreign Aid Policies for Low Income Countries in the 1990s. Institut für Weltwirtschaft, Kiel Discussion Papers, 152, August 1989.

--, Rolf J. LANGHAMMER et al., The Competitive Strength of European, Japanese and US Suppliers on ASEAN Markets. Kieler Studien, 211, Tübingen 1987.

HODARA, Isidoro, Countertrade - Experiences of Some Latin American Countries. UNCTAD Report ST/ECDC/27. Geneva 1985.

HOFFMANN, Stanley, "Reflections on the Nation-State in Western Europe Today". In: Loukas TSOUKALIS (Ed.), The European Community. Past, Present, Future. Oxford 1983, pp. 21-37.

HUGHES, Helen (Ed.), Achieving Industrialization in East Asia. Cambridge, Mass., 1989.

IGUE, Ogunsola John, "Evolution du Commerce Clandestin Entre le Dahomey et le Nigeria Depuis la Guerre du 'Biafra'". Canadian Journal of African Studies, Vol. 10, 1976, pp. 235-257.

--, "L'Officiel, le Parallèle et le Clandestin. Commerces et Intégration en Afrique de l'Ouest". Politique Africaine, No. 9, Paris, March 1983, pp. 29-51.

INOTAI, András, Regional Integration in the New World Economic Environment. Budapest 1986.

JABER, Tayseer A., "The Relevance of Traditional Integration Theory to Less Developed Countries". Journal of Common Market Studies, Vol. 9, 1970, pp. 254-267.

JACKSON, Robert, Carl ROSBERG, Personal Rule in Black Africa. Berkeley 1982.

JERVIS, Robert, "Security Regimes". International Organization, Vol. 36, 1982, pp. 357-378.

JOHNSON, Harry G. [a], Economic Policies Towards Less Developed Countries. Washington 1967.

JOHNSON, Harry G. [b], Money, Trade and Economic Growth. Cambridge 1967.

KAHNERT, Friedrich, P. RICHARDS, E. STOUTJESDIJK, P. THOMO-POULOS, Economic Integration among Developing Countries. OECD Development Centre Studies, Paris 1969.

KEOHANE, Robert O. , "The Demand for International Regimes". International Organization, Vol. 36, 1982, pp. 325-355.

KRASNER, Stephen D. , "Structural Causes and Regime Consequences". International Organization, Vol. 36, 1982, pp. 185-205.

KRAUSS, Melvyn B. , "Recent Developments in Customs Union Theory: An Interpretative Survey". Journal of Economic Literature, Vol. 10, 1972, pp. 413-436.

KREININ, Mordechai E. , "Some Economic Consequences of Reverse Preferences". Journal of Common Market Studies, Vol. 11, 1973, pp. 161-172.

LANGDON, Steven W. , Lynn K. MYTELKA, "Africa in the Changing World Economy". In: Colin LEGUM, I. William ZARTMAN, Steven LANGDON, Lynn K. MYTELKA (Eds.), Africa in the 1980s. New York 1979, pp. 179-188.

LANGHAMMER, Rolf J. , "Regionale Integration zwischen afrikanischen Staaten als Vorbedingung für Exportdiversifizierung?". Die Weltwirtschaft, 1976, No. 1, pp. 132-146.

--, Die Zentralafrikanische Zoll- und Wirtschaftsunion. Integrationswirkungen bei Ländern im Frühstadium der industriellen Entwicklung. Kieler Studien, 151, Tübingen 1978.

--, "The Economic Rationale of Trade Policy Co-operation between ASEAN and the EC: Has Co-operation Benefited ASEAN?". ASEAN Economic Bulletin, Vol. 2, 1985, pp. 107-117.

--, "Tariff Reductions and Tariff Redundancy in ASEAN Countries". ASEAN Economic Bulletin, Vol. 4, 1988, pp. 252-270.

--, Dean SPINANGER, Wirtschaftliche Zusammenarbeit zwischen den Entwicklungsländern. Chancen und Risiken. Kieler Studien, 190, Tübingen 1984.

LEWIS, Arthur W. , "The Slowing Down of the Engine of Growth". The American Economic Review, Vol. 70, 1980, pp. 555-564.

LINDER, Staffan Burenstam, "Customs Unions and Economic Development". In: Miguel S. WIONCZEK (Ed.), Latin American Economic Integration. New York 1966, pp. 32-41.

LIPSEY, Richard G. , "Mr. Gehrels on Customs Unions". The Review of Economic Studies, Vol. 24, 1957, pp. 211-214.

LIPSEY, Richard G., The Theory of Customs Unions: A General Survey". The Economic Journal, Vol. 70, 1960, pp. 496-513.

LITTLE, Ian M.D., "Regional International Companies as an Approach to Economic Integration". Journal of Common Market Studies, Vol. 5, 1966, pp. 181-186.

MACBEAN, Alisdair I., Duc-tho NGUYEN, Commodity Policies: Problems and Prospects. London 1987.

McQUEEN, Matthew, "Lomé and the Protective Effect of Rules of Origin". Journal of World Trade Law, Vol. 16, 1982, No. 2, pp. 119-132.

--, George YANNOPOULOS, ACP Trade: An Urgent Need for an Imaginative and Generous Response by the EC. Lomé Briefing, No. 11, Brussels, October 1989.

MEADE, James E., The Theory of Customs Unions. Amsterdam 1955.

MILNER, Chris R., "Identifying and Quantifying Anti-Export Bias: The Case of Cameroon". Weltwirtschaftliches Archiv, Vol. 126, 1990, pp. 142-155.

MORAWETZ, David, "Extra-Union Exports of Industrial Goods from Customs Unions among Developing Countries". Journal of Development Economics, Vol. 1, 1974, pp. 247-260.

--, Why the Emperor's New Clothes are not Made in Colombia. New York 1981.

MYTELKA, Lynn K., "Foreign Aid and Regional Integration: The UDEAC Case". Journal of Common Market Studies, Vol. 12, 1973, pp. 138-158.

NDONGKO, Wilfred A., "The Economic Origins of the Association of Some African States with the European Economic Community". African Studies Review, Vol. 16, 1973, pp. 219-232.

--, "The Future of the Central African Customs and Economic Union-UDEAC". In: Ralph I. ONWUKA, Amadu SESAY (Eds.), The Future of Regionalism in Africa. New York 1985, pp. 96-109.

NELLIS, John R., Public Enterprises in Sub-Saharan Africa. World Bank Discussion Papers, No. 1, Washington, 1986.

NUGENT, Jeffrey B., Economic Integration in Central America. Baltimore 1974.

NUNNENKAMP, Peter, The International Debt Crisis of the Third World - Causes and Consequences for the World Economy. Brighton 1986.

OECD, Development Performance of Highly Commodity Dependent Developing Countries and Trends in Commodity Markets: A Preliminary Assessment. Paris, January 1989 (mimeo).

ORIMALADE, Adeyinka, R.E. UBOGU (Eds.), Trade and Development in Economic Community of West African States (ECOWAS). New Delhi 1984.

PEARSON, Scott R., William D. INGRAM, "Economies of Scale. Domestic Divergences and Potential Gains from Economic Integration in Ghana and the Ivory Coast". Journal of Political Economy, Vol. 88, 1980, pp. 994-1008.

PELKMANS, Jacques, "The Assignment of Public Functions in Economic Integration". In: Loukas TSOUKALIS (Ed.), The European Community. Past, Present, Future. Oxford 1983, pp. 97-121.

--, "The Institutional Economics of European Integration". In: M. CAPELLETTI et al. (Eds.), Integration Through Law. Vol. 1, Book 1, Berlin 1986, pp. 318-396.

PSACHAROPOULOS, George, "Returns to Education: An Updated International Comparison". In: Timothy KING (Ed.), Education and Income. World Bank Staff Working Paper, No. 402, Washington, D.C., July 1980, pp. 75-109.

RAMSETT, David E., Regional Industrial Development in Central America: A Case Study of the Integration Industries Scheme. New York 1969.

RAVENHILL, John, "The Future of Regionalism in Africa". In: Ralph I. ONWUKA, Amadu SESAY (Eds.), The Future of Regionalism in Africa. New York 1985, pp. 205-224.

RIEGER, Hans Christoph, ASEAN Co-operation and Intra-ASEAN Trade. Institute of Southeast Asean Studies, Research Notes and Discussion Paper No. 57, Singapore 1985.

ROBSON, Peter, Economic Integration in Africa. London 1968.

--, Integration, Development and Equity. Economic Integration in West Africa. London 1983.

--, "Regional Integration and the Crisis in Sub-Saharan Africa". Journal of Modern African Studies, Vol. 23, 1985, pp. 603-611.

SANCHEZ, Aurora (Ed.), Non-Tariff Barriers and Trade in ASEAN. ASEAN Economic Bulletin, Special Focus, Vol. 4, Singapore 1987, No. 1.

SANDBROOK, Richard, The Politics of Africa's Economic Stagnation. Cambridge 1985.

--, "The State and Economic Stagnation in Tropical Africa". World Development, Vol. 14, 1986, pp. 319-332.

SAWYER, Charles W., Richard L. SPRINKLE, "Alternative Empirical Estimates of Trade Creation and Trade Diversion: A Comparison of the Baldwin-Murray and Verdoorn Models". Weltwirtschaftliches Archiv, Vol. 125, 1989, pp. 61-73.

SECRETARIA PERMANENTE DEL TRATADO GENERAL DE INTEGRACION ECONOMICA CENTROAMERICANA (SIECA), Carta Informativa. Guatemala, August 1971.

SEGAL, Aaron, "The Integration of Developing Countries: Some Thoughts on East Africa and Central America". Journal of Common Market Studies, Vol. 5, 1967, pp. 252-282.

SOPIEE, Noordin, Chew Lay SEE, Lim Siang JIN (Eds.), ASEAN at the Crossroads: Obstacles, Options and Opportunities in Economic Co-operation. Kuala Lumpur 1987.

TYERS, Rodney, Kym ANDERSON, "Liberalising OECD Agricultural Policies in the Uruguay Round: Effects on Trade and Welfare". Journal of Agricultural Economics, Vol. 39, 1988, pp. 197-216.

UNCTAD [a], Handbook of International Trade and Development Statistics. New York, various issues.

-- [b], Major New Developments in the Economic Co-operation and Integration Groupings of Developing Countries (1985-87). TD/B/C/87, Geneva, 6 July 1988.

-- [c], Review of Developments in the Area of Trade and Monetary and Financial Co-operation among Developing Countries. TD/B/C.7/92, Geneva, 29 March 1989.

-- [d], Trade Expansion and Economic Integration among Developing Countries. TD/B/85/Rev. 1, New York 1967.

UNITED NATIONS (UN), "Economic Co-operation among Member Countries of the Association of Southeast Asian Nations: Report of a United Nations Team". Journal of Development Planning, No. 7, United Nations, New York 1974.

--, Statistical Papers, Series D, Commodity Trade Statistics, Vol. 31, 1981, Fasc. 18, New York 1982.

--, Statistical Papers, Series D, Commodity Trade Statistics, Vol. 35, 1985, Fasc. 14, New York 1987.

--, Financing Africa's Recovery. Report and Recommendations of the Advisory Group on Financial Flows for Africa. New York, 1988.

VAITSOS, Constantine V., "The Crisis in Economic Co-operation among Developing Countries". World Development, Vol. 6, 1978, pp. 719-769.

VALDES, Alberto, Joachim ZIETZ, Agricultural Protection in OECD Countries: Its Cost to Less-Developed Countries. Research Report 21, International Food Policy Research Institute, Washington, D.C., 1980.

VINER, Jacob, The Customs Union Issue. New York 1950.

WILFORD, Walton T., "Trade Creation in the Central American Common Market". Western Economic Journal, Vol. 8, 1970, pp. 61-69.

WILLMORE, Larry, "Free Trade in Manufactures among Developing Countries: The Central American Experience". Economic Development and Cultural Change, Vol. 20, 1972, pp. 659-670.

--, "The Pattern of Trade and Specialization in the Central American Common Market". Journal of Economic Studies, Vol. 1, 1974, pp. 113-134.

--, "Trade Creation, Trade Diversion and Effective Protection in the Central American Common Market". Journal of Development Studies, Vol. 12, 1976, pp. 396-414.

--, "The Industrial Economics of Intra-Industry Trade and Specialization". In: Herbert GIERSCH (Ed.), On the Economics of Intra-Industry Trade. Symposium 1978. Tübingen 1979, pp. 185-205.

WIONCZEK, Miguel S., "The Central American Common Market". In: Peter ROBSON (Ed.), International Economic Integration, Selected Readings. Harmondsworth 1972.

WOGART, Jan P., Industrialization in Colombia. Policies, Patterns, Perspectives. Kieler Studien, 153, Tübingen 1978.

--, José Silvero MARQUES, "Trade Liberalisation, Tariff Redundancy and Inflation. A Methodological Exploration Applied to Argentina". Weltwirtschaftliches Archiv, Vol. 121, 1985, pp. 18-39.

WORLD BANK, Price Prospects for Major Commodities. Washington, D.C., 1986.

--, World Development Report 1987. New York 1987.

-- [1988a], Adjustment Lending - An Evaluation of Ten Years of Experience. Policy Research Series, No. 1, Washington, D.C., 1988.

-- [1988b], World Development Report 1988. New York 1988.

-- [1988c], Intra-Regional Trade in Sub-Saharan Africa. Trade and Finance Division, Technical Department, Africa Region, Washington, D.C., 30 December 1988 (mimeo).

-- [1989a], Trade Liberalization and Economic Integration in Central America. Report No. 7625-CAM, Washington, D.C., 10 March 1989.

--[1989b], World Development Report 1989. New York 1989.

YONDO, Marcel, Dimension Nationale et Développement Economique. Théorie - Application dans l'UDEAC. Paris 1970.

ZEHENDER, Wolfgang, Cooperation versus Integration: The Prospects of the Southern African Development Coordination Conference (SADCC). Berlin 1983.

ZEHENDER, Wolfgang, Regional Cooperation Through Trade and Industry? The Prospects of Regional Economic Communities in West and Central Africa. Berlin 1987.

Institut für Weltwirtschaft an der Universität Kiel

The Completion of the Internal Market Symposium 1989

Edited by Horst Siebert. Tübingen 1990. VII, 387 pages.
Paper DM 82.–, ISBN 3-16-145567-3. Cloth DM 107.–, ISBN 3-16-145568-1.

I. GENERAL ISSUES

1992: Are the Figures Right? Reflections of a Thirty Per Cent Policy Maker, J. Waelbroeck

An Alternative Assessment of the Macro-Economic Effects of "Europe 1992", A. F. Bakhoven – Discussants of both papers: M. Emerson, D. Lal

The Harmonization Issue in Europe: Prior Agreement or a Competitive Process?, H. Siebert – Discussants: G. Prosi, R. Scheid

Regulation and the Single Market: An Economic Perspective, J. Pelkmans – Discussant: H. Willgerodt

II. SECTORAL AND SPATIAL ASPECTS

Implications for the Reform of the CAP, U. Koester – Discussant: J.-V. Schrader

Institutional Requirements for a Common Market in Transport Services, H.-J. Ewers – Discussant: J. Müller

Will the Completion of the Internal Market Lead to Regional Divergence?, W. T. M. Molle

III. INTERNATIONAL REPERCUSSIONS

The Competition of the Internal Market: Growth Locomotive or Fortress Europe?, S. Ostry

The Creation of the EC Internal Market and Its Effects on the Competitiveness of Producers in Other Industrial Economies, G. Eliasson, L. Lundberg – Discussant of both papers: A. Erdilek

1992 and Its Implications for Developing Countries, V. Cable – Discussant: D. Lal

Eastern Europe: Challenge of 1992 Dwarfed by Pressures of System's Decline, J. Winiecki – Discussant: B. Kádár

IV. FINANCIAL MARKETS AND MONETARY ASPECTS

The Path to Financial Integration in Europe, P. Minford – Discussant: N. Walter

The Benefits and Costs of Currency Unification, N. Thygesen – Discussants: H. G. Grubel, H. Willgerodt

J. C. B. Mohr (Paul Siebeck) Tübingen
Postfach 20 40, D-7400 Tübingen

Kieler Studien

Institut für Weltwirtschaft an der Universität Kiel

Herausgegeben von Horst Siebert
Schriftleitung: Hubertus Müller-Groeling

220. Henning Klodt et al., Forschungspolitik unter EG-Kontrolle. 1988. X, 141 S. Broschiert *DM* 47,—. Leinen *DM* 67,—.

221. Bernhard Fischer, Peter Nunnenkamp et al., Capital-Intensive Industries in Newly Industrializing Countries: The Case of the Brazilian Automobile and Steel Industries. 1988. XVII, 325 S. Broschiert *DM* 74,—. Leinen *DM* 94,—.

222. Heike Göbel, Rolf J. Langhammer, Frank D. Weiss, Wachstum im asiatisch-pazifischen Raum. Implikationen für die internationale Arbeitsteilung. 1988. XII, 199 S. Broschiert *DM* 64,—. Leinen *DM* 84,—.

223. Federico Foders, Rüdiger Wolfrum et al., Meereswirtschaft in Europa. Rechtliche und ökonomische Rahmenbedingungen für deutsche Unternehmen. 1989. XIV, 317 S. Broschiert *DM* 88,—. Leinen *DM* 108,—.

224. Konrad Lammers, Regionalförderung und Schiffbausubventionen in der Bundesrepublik. 1989. XI, 207 S. Broschiert *DM* 79,—. Leinen *DM* 99,—.

225. Uwe Corsepius, Kapitalmarktreform in Entwicklungsländern. Eine Analyse am Beispiel Perus. 1989. XIII, 212 S. Broschiert *DM* 79,—. Leinen *DM* 99,—.

226. Adrian Bothe, Die Gemeindeausgaben in der Bundesrepublik. Ein nachfrageorientierter Erklärungsansatz. 1989. IX, 154 S. Broschiert *DM* 63,—. Leinen *DM* 83,—.

227. Torsten Amelung, Die Politische Ökonomie der Importsubstitution und der Handelsliberalisierung. Das Beispiel Türkei. 1989. XIV, 259 S. Broschiert *DM* 78,—. Leinen *DM* 98,—.

228. Henning Klodt, Klaus-Dieter Schmidt et al., Weltwirtschaftlicher Strukturwandel und Standortwettbewerb. Die deutsche Wirtschaft auf dem Prüfstand. 1989. XVI, 219 S. Broschiert *DM* 69,—. Leinen *DM* 89,—.

229. Uwe Corsepius, Peter Nunnenkamp, Rainer Schweickert, Debt versus Equity Finance in Developing Countries: An Empirical Analysis of the Agent-Principal Model of International Capital Transfers. 1989. XI, 128 S. Broschiert *DM* 52,—. Leinen *DM* 72,—.

230. Erich Gundlach, Joachim Scheide, Stefan Sinn, Die Entwicklung nationaler Auslandsvermögenspositionen. Konsequenzen für die Wirtschaftspolitik. 1990. X, 137 S. Broschiert *DM* 55,—. Leinen *DM* 78,—.

231. Matthias Lücke, Traditional Labour-Intensive Industries in Newly Industrializing Countries: The Case of Brazil. 1990. XV, 214 S. Broschiert *DM* 62,—. Leinen *DM* 85,—.

232. Rolf J. Langhammer, Ulrich Hiemenz, Regional Integration among Developing Countries: Opportunities, Obstacles and Options. 1990. IX, 102 S. Broschiert *DM* 49,—.

J.C.B. Mohr (Paul Siebeck) Tübingen

Postfach 2040, D-7400 Tübingen
ISSN 0340 - 6989